Alan Abernet

Fulfilment and Frustration
MINISTRY IN TODAY'S CHURCH

the columba press

First published in 2002 by
ᴄʜᴇ ᴄᴏʟᴜᴍʙᴀ ᴘʀᴇꜱꜱ
55A Spruce Avenue, Stillorgan Industrial Park,
Blackrock, Co Dublin

Cover by Bill Bolger
Origination by The Columba Press
Printed in Ireland by ColourBooks Ltd, Dublin

ISBN 1 85607 358 0

Contents

CHAPTER ONE

The Beginnings

In the midst of constant activity and the ministry of doing, it has been difficult to reflect upon my vocation and to examine what has been happening at deep inner levels of the mind and the spirit. The reflections that follow are an attempt to make sense of my own journey of faith in the context of vocation to ordained ministry. There are many particular facets to these thoughts: biographical detail, events, people, situations and at the core of my thoughts the struggle with personal faith and public ministry. I begin at the point where the kernel of my own struggle began. This is the place where faith, church and life impinged upon each other in a profound way in the life of a six year old child.

The details of that day are very sketchy in my memory, although I do remember it was cloudy and dry. This was the second of two primary schools I had attended. Harding Memorial Primary School has a special place in my mind. For me the opportunity to play football was a major part of my pleasure. It also made a big difference when the football coach was my teacher for my last two years in the school. From an early age I thought I would be a primary school teacher. Things obviously took a different turn.

Let me return to that cloudy day. My brother and I had set out for school as normal, assuming we would return home that evening. I was never to see the inside of that house again. We were collected from school and brought to my grandparents' house, which was next door to the school. We could walk out of the back door of my grandparents' home and be at one of the school gates. We were to live here for a few years.

Others tell the details of this part of my life to me. I never heard the full story from my mum as she took her secrets to her grave. She was a remarkable and special lady. My father for some time had been gambling very heavily and he had managed to work his way through the family inheritance he had received. On that particular day the bailiffs had arrived at our home to inform my mum that she had lost her home because of my father's debts. She took the two of us to her parents' home that was a few streets away. We had moved to the home we lost that day only a short time before, as it was smaller than our previous home which had been sold to ease the difficulties which were already evident.

I cannot begin to imagine what this must have been like for my mum. She was already in her late forties by this stage, having married relatively late in life. She now was left with no home, two young children, no job and the public disgrace. It may have been different now but the stigma then was immense. As well as all these difficulties I gather she was paying off some of my father's debts for some time to come. My father disappeared. I remember seeing him on two occasions after that day. He took the two of us out for the afternoon but more than that I cannot remember.

The part of the story that is most relevant to my journey is that the church was unable to help her. To be separated or divorced was something that damaged religious credibility, especially in this land of saints and scholars. People did not know how to handle this moral dilemma. Her reputation was in tatters and it was not possible then to be a member of the Mother's Union if you were separated or divorced. Mercifully things have changed, but my mum, at a critical moment in her life, did not find the acceptance and compassion of Christ's people. The religious culture of this troubled land found it very difficult to cope when things did not conform to the rules and regulations of the religious club. Sometimes I fear that the law of faith is much more important than the wonderful freedom of grace. I believe that the law of scripture shows us that all of us are in need of grace. This is a grace that accepts people and does not condemn them. This is also a grace that does not judge people but draws alongside to support and help.

The great miracle of this situation was my mum's strong, personal and gentle faith, a faith that remained unassuming, humble and thankful for what she had. This was a faith that taught me not to speak of what I did not have but of what I did have. For her, faith helped her in what must have at times been a lonely road, to find the Lord's love and presence. It was also a faith that enabled her to die in peace. There is no doubt in my mind, having watched her die, that death came as a friend. From a faithful and loving mum I learned to see God, especially in the difficult times. For that moulding and influence I am and I will be forever grateful.

Much of my own story that follows began as a child watching my mum do more than just cope. She was able to be generous and kind with the little she had. She was able to pick herself up and give unstintingly to the two of us. Her pain did not make her cynical and bitter. She never told me the full story of what had happened, only that my dad had been a sick man and that gambling was to be avoided at all costs. She also had an enormous aversion to lies of any shape or form. The worst crime we could commit was to tell her a lie.

Therefore from an early age I learned to have faith but I also learned that life could be painful and difficult. Having faith was no guarantee that all would be well. My own faith was shaped by those who loved me most, but also by the circumstances of my life. From an early stage of my development this included what I like to refer to as a healthy disrespect for the institutional church. I have to confess that there are times still when this disrespect feels more like intense anger. An anger that found it difficult to accept how someone with such a strong and personal faith was made to feel so inadequate in her faith.

It was unusual in the early 60s not to have the nuclear family. I always felt the exception in my school not to have a dad at home. There were times when it was both uncomfortable and embarrassing. It was usually easier not to mention it and hope that people would not ask.

There is a danger in this story being recounted that it may appear I had an unhappy childhood and that my young life was full of difficult events and pain. There were difficulties but there were also some very special people and gifts that helped the process of growing up to be full of love and support.

My mum's family were very supportive and even protective. My aunts and uncles would ensure that we had holidays, special presents and lots of love. My uncle Ivor and auntie Dora deserve a special mention; they are two ordinary and yet extraordinary people. They simply live their lives without fuss or looking for recognition but are amazingly generous and thoughtful. They were always there for me and I know they always will be.

The person who influenced me most, other than my mum, was my 'poppy'. My grandfather was a quiet man (my granny tended to make up for him) who loved his family and his football. He had the misfortune of being a Manchester City supporter. My brother and I had to be different and also because of George Best, we supported Manchester United. There are those who would say I am a fanatic. I must simply state that I was one of those 40,000 fans who were in Barcelona the night we won the European Cup in 1999.

His influence is immeasurable. He lived his faith and would not talk about it unless he was asked. There were no sermons or great testimony of faith but a love and strength that came from his deep faith. I do remember once when I was a teenager asking him about his early experiences and he told me how influenced he was by the legendary W. P. Nicholson whom he heard preach in Belfast. He worshipped regularly and served his local parish church by counting the freewill offering every week. He is now rejoicing upon another shore and yet his presence and influence are still with me.

The one story I tell to illustrate his wisdom still profoundly affects how I think about others and, hopefully, how I treat them. During those first few years after my father disappeared we lived with my grandparents. One of my reactions to the trauma of what had happened with my parents was to steal. I usually stole from my granny's purse. One particular day before I had gone to school I stole a coin from my granny's purse. It was her 'kitty' purse used for messages and bills. It was kept in the bottom drawer of the sideboard in the living room

When I came home from school my poppy came to my bedroom and told me he knew I had taken the money. He then asked me to put it back as he was going out to do a message. Thankfully I hadn't spent the money and I was able to put it back in the purse. Later that night he came into my bedroom and thanked me for putting it back. He told me he would never tell anyone what I had done and hoped I wouldn't do it again. He also added that he loved me and that he forgave me. Until the day he died, which was more than ten years later, he never again mentioned that moment and he never told my mum. Years later I asked her about the incident and she knew nothing about it.

For me this was and is a modern day parable. In my thinking it is a parallel to the story of the 'forgiving father' of Luke 15. I believe the emphasis in this story is meant to be on the father who forgives the son. I quote from N. T. Wright:

The father himself was being reckless, prodigal, generous to a fault…. For the younger brother to ask for his share of the inheritance is almost unthinkable: it is the functional equivalent of saying to his father, 'I wish you were dead.' The father should have beaten him or thrown him out. Instead he agrees. The son ends up doing the job beyond which it was impossible, in Jewish eyes, to sink: feeding pigs for a gentile master. He then does a further unthinkable thing: he returns home, threatening to disgrace the whole family in the eyes of the village. The father runs to meet him; senior members of families never do anything so undignified at the best of times, let alone in order to greet someone who should have remained in self imposed ignominy. (*Jesus and the Victory of God*, page 129, par 1.)

Unlike my mum's experience of legalistic religion, I was accepted, loved and forgiven. The irony in my mind is particularly poignant: I had sinned but was forgiven and accepted; my mum had been unfortunate to marry a man who was sick yet did not experience the same compassion.

This moment early in my life highlights something of the faith I was given as a gift by my family through some particularly unfortunate circumstances, a faith that was deeply personal and yet intensely private; a faith that has at its heart an awareness of God who is always present with us at all times but especially in the pain.

This awareness of God was in contrast to unease with the church. This unease was not helped by my experience of church as a child and as a teenager, when I had the feeling I did not belong. To belong you had to be an adult and preferably middle aged or older. This struggle was complicated by the fact that my own questioning took place within the context of the 'Troubles'. As my faith and vocation were to develop I also had an increasing frustration with the narrow definitions of faith that appeared to leave no room for doubt. It also did not allow for those who differed from you in religious thinking and most certainly did not allow for the possibility that sometimes I might just be wrong. There was what I can only describe as a Pharisaic mindset that was self righteous and harsh in what passed for religious fervour and thought.

Increasingly in reading scripture, in being with others who have found faith, and in being with others who struggle with faith, I have found the analogy of faith as a journey very helpful. This gives a three dimensional aspect to faith. There is a past, a present and a future. Along the way there may be wrong turnings, cul-de-sacs, mountaintop and dark valley experiences. All these go to make up a rich tapestry of faith that is held together by a firm conviction that the Lord is with us always.

Throughout the Book of Psalms we find the integrity and honesty of faith expressed in many different moods. Under girding all these experiences and human responses is a faith that is rooted in past experience by the individual and the community.

In my late teenage years I found church increasingly difficult. It was stiff, formal, and unhelpful and it jarred with my own journey. I wanted joy, freedom and spontaneity to be the core of my expression of faith. I experimented with different Christian groups. However, I could not get away from the fact that this church which I found difficult had also been such an important part of why I had found faith. The great paradox of my journey, I found this church infuriating yet it had brought me so much. This same church had given me the gift of community among my peers and the challenge of personal faith. I could not escape from this paradox and it has been part of my struggle ever since.

From the inheritance my family has given me as a gift, and by those who prayed for me and supported me, the shoots of vocation have grown. Those who showed me the loveliness of Jesus have prepared the way for growth to take place. That vocation has always been a reluctant one and found the experiences of church and religious life in our community a constant threat to it.

Vocation as I have experienced it and witnessed it in others can often have tension at the heart of it – the tentative belief that God is calling, the willingness to go but also the unwillingness to be part of the institutional church that can at times appear to hide Jesus. This institution of the church causes great frustration to those who serve within it, but it also gives the channels for people to find great fulfilment in being a servant of the servant king.

As I reflect upon these early years of my life and my own journey of faith, I am left acknowledging two gifts that are at the heart of my vocation. The first is the gift of faith. The second is the struggle with the institutional church and religion that can so easily become legalistic, cold and devoid of compassion. These gifts are still the backbone of my faith, vocation and ministry. They are what have compelled me to write about ministry in today's church. For the first gift I am forever grateful; for the second gift I am learning to see it as a gift.

CHAPTER 2

To be or not to be

With my early negative thinking towards the church, my vocational journey was not one of procrastination but reluctance. All through my childhood I had found church frustrating. Church activities were at the centre of my recreational and social life. There was the Boy's Brigade and then I became the infamous traitor when I left them and joined the Boy Scouts. They were less formal, had more sport and the outdoor life of camping and mountaineering. Within church life there was also time for Sunday school, Bible class, and as I got older, confirmation, Christian Endeavour, youth club and youth fellowship. These in different ways sought to mould me in my faith.

The highlight of all the activities was the wonderful lazy and fun-filled summers playing tennis. We were very fortunate in my home parish in the city of Belfast to have our own tennis courts. Morning, afternoon and evenings, senior members permitting, were spent playing tennis and hanging out together. To this day I still love playing tennis. All these church activities for young people were so important. There was so much fun and crack. We were a diverse group of young people who made up the youth scene.

There was a great sense of belonging. We were a community, a gang, a bunch of young people who were simply given the opportunity to meet together. I am not sure we felt part of the church, as we were distanced from what happened every Sunday and were usually blamed for any damage done to the church property by some of the older members of the congregation. However, we were given the space and the place to be together.

Summer camps were also an important part of my faith journey. These were times when I belonged to an enlarged family for a week every summer. The fun, fellowship and practical jokes made these camps special. The local young girls may have been an added attraction. The concept of fun and faith belonging together was and is very important to me. I did not want faith to mean I became a killjoy or lost my sense of fun. Faith for me, then and now, was not about rules and regulations. It should not be about the hardening of the 'oughteries' as Gerard Hughes describes this legalistic type of faith in his book, *God of Surprises*.

These camps also had leaders and campers from all over Ireland. They were held in Sutton or Greystones, north or south Dublin. This was very useful for a young person from Northern Ireland to meet people and experience life beyond the border.

In between these camps I found it very hard to live out my faith in the environment of school and I missed the support of the people I had while at camp. My faith would often seem to disappear altogether, not in the sense of believing but in seeking every day to follow Jesus. I found it difficult to engage with God in these years especially when I did not find church helpful. Church was a place where I had no voice or any chance to express my faith in a helpful medium.

In fact there is one moment when I felt the harshness of religion and church profoundly. I was sitting at the back of the church during a Sunday evening service with a friend. I was dressed properly in jacket, shirt and tie; even as a teenager this was the accepted dress code. We were admittedly chatting quietly through a very tedious sermon, not that I can remember any of the detail. Then suddenly the churchwarden asked us to move to the front of the church. We complied with this request rather meekly and he walked with us to the front pew and left us sitting there for the remainder of the sermon, which seemed to take forever. We were so stunned that we did as we were asked. If it happened now I am sure we would have simply walked out of church and not come back. The part of this that I find most difficult is that nobody said they thought this was wrong or even a

little over the top. The good news is that I have not had a problem with churchwardens since then, although I do get to choose
one of them.

The church in my childhood and youth was about being
quiet. It was about children and young people being seen and
not heard. I suppose you could argue very cynically that it
worked, in that many of my generation are now not seen or
heard in church today.

It was during my last year of school that my faith became
more clear and purposeful. The future was uncertain and I was
unclear what I wanted to do when I left school. I thought I
would like to teach but was not sure where to train or what to
teach. At the same time my poppy was ill and suffering from another stroke. He had been my surrogate dad, a loving and wise
friend. Questions concerning life and death, meaning and purpose, suddenly became very important. With the mixture of so
many emotions at a very important time in my life there was the
need for a much clearer focus and purpose for my life.

At this time, in my own parish of Willowfield, there was a
week of special activities for teenagers. Each evening I listened
and was challenged. The speaker was from the Church Army,
David Griscome, now ordained and serving in the Church of
Ireland. I wanted to go into the future knowing that Jesus was
with me. I wanted to 'go for it' and see where God might lead
me.

This was a formative moment in my vocational journey.
Despite feeling the church had let my mum down and had not
given me a voice, at a critical point in my journey it had helped
me face the future and re-ignite my faith.

Things then happened rapidly. I soon was a Sunday school
teacher, youth club leader and youth fellowship leader. Within
eighteen months I had preached my first sermon. I remember it
very clearly. It was based on Psalm 46 verse 10: 'Be still and
know that I am God.' People were beginning to suggest that I
should be ordained. The vocation that I was beginning to feel
was being recognised by those who knew me. I was given op-

portunities to test and express it. I believe that it is critical to have vocation tested and affirmed, especially within the local Christian community.

During this stage of my journey there was also the challenge of meeting people beyond the boundaries which I had as a child and as a young person. The mixture of faiths and no faiths in university life was fascinating. My particular challenge was to move beyond my Protestant boundaries. I had been brought up in a home where religious affiliation did not make a difference to how we should treat people. However, in my home community people had been bombed out of their homes because of where they worshipped. I had also watched the local Catholic church be desecrated by gangs of people who carried out such deeds in the name of 'God and Ulster'. I know this happened on both sides of the divide and there are many such stories. However, these events left me wondering where is Jesus in the midst of all this? What would he make of such violence and mayhem?

My student days made me cross previously unrecognised boundaries. I was to find a very good friend called Brendan in one of my classes. We talked, we shared, we laughed and we discussed our faith stories. He worshipped in a different church, he held different political aspirations and he was a good guy. I could use the typical and offensive Northern Ireland phrase: 'He was a nice guy but he was a Catholic.' How awful that sounds but how true it has been of our culture and thinking. This is a way of separating people and excluding others because of an innate prejudice. We are all made in the image of God.

The most intriguing part of this friendship was that we were both seeking to follow Jesus. So we went to worship in each other's churches. I found myself tackling this issue as I sat in his church on Ash Wednesday. The symbolism and the liturgical significance of ashes were explained to me. It was wonderful biblical theology but I had assumed that because they did it, it must be wrong.

These and other issues started to make me ask real questions about my faith that had assumptions that excluded and judged others so easily. This was to become an important part of my vocational journey. Where someone worshipped was not the important issue. As I followed Jesus he would lead me into new places where I would learn new lessons. As he was with me, I had nothing to fear.

As time past I went to the Churches Advisory Council for The Ministry, CACTM. It was a very positive experience of shared worship, communal meals and focused interviews. The interviews ranged from questions about spirituality, academic interest, psychological make up and then some from a lay perspective.

They recommended me for ordination on condition that I finished my university course. The years at Queen's gave me great experience in leading small groups and handling various leadership responsibilities. My politics tutorials were to give me great experience for the future. It was important to keep your arguments to the point with a good beginning and a very concise ending. The lesson would prove invaluable when it came to preaching.

So I left Queen's and found myself living away from home in Dublin, a new world of experiences and friendship opening up before me. I started my training for ordination.

Much has been said about the ordination training in the Church of Ireland. Many of the comments have been negative and at times unnecessarily personal. This is not the place to make any comments on my training. However, I do wonder how wise it is to train clergy in a community environment where students often feel they are in a boarding school rather than in a theological college. Training people for ministry would be more much more meaningful in a situation of doing ministry. I want to return to this subject in a later chapter.

I made wonderful friends in college and I enjoyed student life in Trinity College. I also met the love of my life in Dublin, Liz, later to become my wife. In college it was good to relate to people from a different church background and whose faith journey was not the same. These moments of sharing, of conflict and disagreement, of causing pain and apologising, were formative in the vocational journey.

As a good evangelical Protestant from the north, I protested about the lighting of the candles in the college chapel. The warden asked me to listen to the views of someone who found them a helpful symbol that enriched their worship. A compromise was reached when it was decided that the candles would only be lit on certain occasions. I am embarrassed by my arrogance as I remember the incident, but ironically I now find candles a very helpful symbol in my own prayers.

To learn from others, and especially from those we may not agree with, was to become an important aspect of my faith journey ever since.

The final year in college was full of the usual difficulties of trying to discover where I would serve as a curate. The decision was eventually made and it was to be St Elizabeth's Dundonald, on the outskirts of East Belfast. I had been baptised in the old church in Dundonald and had lived there until I was five. The beginning of my father's difficulties meant the family home being sold and we moved to Belfast. I attributed this first parish to a divine sense of humour as the prodigal son was returning home. It certainly made the choice of passage for my first sermon easy.

Before the big day in Down Cathedral, there were various things that highlighted my own struggle with this moment in my life. The fitting out in clerical gear was a strange sensation. My robes, the new suit and the clerical shirt all had to be purchased and modelled for my friends and family. The first time I looked in the mirror and saw myself in a clerical collar the emotions were mixed and confused. The finality of ordination struck a very deep chord in my spirit. I can still feel the fear as I envisaged the enormity of what I was doing. What if I couldn't hack it? What if I wasn't happy? What if I just couldn't do it? What else could I do?

These negative emotions were part of my psyche and from my childhood I knew what fear was. I knew that when things were going well that was the time to worry. There was always bad just waiting around the corner. So I approached my ordination with a huge internal struggle. I knew I was meant to do it, although that is difficult to explain. I also did not want to become part of this institution that I despised.

This turmoil was to come to a head when Liz and I travelled to London for her sister's twenty-first birthday party. Hazel was training to be a nurse in St Bartholomew's hospital in London. The party was after I finished college but before ordination.

The three of us found ourselves in the small chapel in the grounds of the hospital. It was a small stone chapel and simply furnished. We sat in the back row of this quiet place of prayer. The turmoil within had been growing and they prayed with me. As they did so there was an overwhelming sense of peace that filled my spirit. The words that came to mind were unusual as they are often associated with endings rather than beginnings: 'Lord, now let your servant go in peace.' Those words have been special to me ever since. I was being forced to face my fear and could only go forward to ordination knowing what I learned as a child. No matter what was going to happen, he promised to be with me. This was all I had, there were no guarantees other than that. There was no map and no certainties as to where I might be led. Even at the beginning of ministry the paradox was present: I would not find the fulfilment of ministry without welcoming the frustration.

The call to ordination for me was not about being at peace but about finding peace in the turmoil. That is my experience ever since. The fulfilment is made the more special by the frustrations that are always present. The frustrations can be coped with much easier if there are enough moments of fulfilment and affirmation. As my ordained ministry began there was at the centre a paradox and this is what had made my vocation possible in the first place.

CHAPTER 3

The Unresolved Questions

There was a huge adjustment from student life to employment. The carefree student days of being in charge of your own life and diary gave way to self-discipline, long working hours and fewer holidays. Very quickly there were unresolved questions facing me in this new life that were made more difficult by the way other adjustments had to be made as I got used to wearing a dog collar.

The new job included somewhere new to live. It also meant living in a new community and meeting a sea of faces who all knew who I was as they had been expecting my arrival. It was strange moving from living in a religious community to living on my own. I did not mind leaving behind the confines of college – I am not sure I was meant to live in community. Having breakfast, lunch, dinner and supper with the same people every day was not the ideal environment for adult education, or at least not for me. This combined with regular compulsory prayers every day for three years meant it was not difficult to want to move to the next chapter of ministry. I was glad to find my own space, to cook my own food and to have my own privacy.

Privacy was of course a relative matter. The new curate certainly appeared to cause interest in the local area and I always felt that I was being watched. On reflection, I am sure people were just being friendly. I had to adjust to being public property. Starting a new job is one thing, but adapting to living on the job and being available all the time was an added pressure and adjustment.

There were many times in college when I resented having to say my prayers when somebody told me to. I now found myself

missing the fellowship and discipline. I was now the professional
and praying was part of the job. My own spiritual journey to this
point had taught me the value of the 'quiet time'. This is a particular evangelical inheritance. This is 'a pattern of daily devotion
involving mainly prayer and Bible reading, conducted at a time
suited to the individual, though usually first thing in the morning before the activities of the day.' (*Not of This World*, Glen
Jordan, page 53.) The praying involved in this particular devotion especially focused on intercessory prayer or in praying for
others. As a student I had sought to be diligent in following this
discipline but very quickly I found it was just not adequate. Any
Bible reading I did was quickly deflected from personal devotion to how this material could be used for the weekly sermon or
Bible study group. I quickly started to search for other ways to
enrich or deepen the spiritual life that was at the heart of my
vocation. The spirituality of other traditions was to become a
helpful resource. My spiritual life needed to be tended, guarded
and developed. The tools I had been given were never going to
help me survive the journey ahead. One of the contributors to
Glen Jordan's study says: 'What spirituality I got from evangeli-
calism, the quiet time and so on, had run out on me. I found it
was not enough for the hard slog of ministry. I had to look beyond that into the spirituality of other traditions.'

There was an obvious difficulty in this part of my struggle. I
was wondering was I being unfaithful to my evangelical roots.
In the minds of some people who came from the same background, I was probably becoming too ecumenical or liberal. The
religious world of our country can sometimes be about control
and guilt rather than about freedom and experimentation. I was
beginning to look at areas of spirituality such as meditation,
journals, retreats, spiritual direction and liturgy. Some of these
tools might be considered suspect in some quarters. I wanted to
ensure this relationship with Jesus was kept fresh and vibrant.
The idea of being on a journey with him was becoming much
more meaningful than any idea of having arrived at the destination.

These various disciplines were to prove of great benefit. Richard Foster's book, *The Celebration of Discipline*, was enormously helpful and inspiring. He helped me see this journey as exciting and he encouraged people in their journeys to experiment. He writes: 'One of the liberating experiences in my life came when I understood that prayer involved a learning process. I was set free to question, to experiment, even to fail, for I knew that I was learning.' (page 33.) This relationship needed to be nurtured and different things would be of help to different people. I was able to try new things, to change my quiet time from something that induced guilt to something that could let me dare and experiment. At a critical time in the development of ministry these concepts were to bring me a new sense of joy in the journey. I will discuss some of these disciplines in a later chapter.

The need to help the interior life was particularly important because I was being thrown very quickly into the full force of pastoral crises. Throughout my early years of theological training, I believed I would be able to answer almost any difficult questions about faith and belief. I had that delightful arrogance of youthful enthusiasm. My worldview at this point in my life meant that I believed God sent everything to us and he was always in control of all events. I had rationalised my own childhood experiences into believing that what happened to us as a family led me to ordination.

These thoughts and ideas were sent into free fall by one of my first pastoral crises. My rector was on holiday and a young sixteen-year-old boy committed suicide by adding some cyanide to his soft drink. I found myself arriving at that devastated household in the early hours of the morning. I was sleepy and did not know any of the details until I got there. There was nothing of value I could say to shell-shocked and grieving parents. Their world had fallen apart and I was struggling with their raw pain and my own inadequacy. There are certainly no slick and pious answers to this mess. Well, there were probably some people who would want to offer empty religious clichés but mercifully even I knew how inappropriate they would be. I can still feel the emptiness, the waste, and the confusion and to this day there is a family living with that pain. In my own mind I could sense anger with God. They were not aware of anything but trying simply to survive the profound and inexplicable pain.

The questions surrounding suffering and pain were to imprint themselves upon my mind. Did God send this tragedy? Is this what God wanted for such a young life? In fact, where was God in this hell? Questions such as these do not have answers. Nothing can take away the pain of human suffering. This was the real struggle of pastoral ministry that nothing could have prepared me for. These questions are still with me but the search for answers has become less important because I do not believe there are any answers. The Book of Job is sometimes said to answer the question of suffering. However, I agree with Phillip Yancey on this matter. He believes that Job does not answer the question of suffering but only gives us clues.

Shortly after this tragedy came another sudden and terrible death. She was eighteen and riding pillion on a motorbike. A freak accident as a horse came out in front of them. Her parents rushed to hospital and they saw her briefly before she was taken to theatre. They never saw her alive again as she died from her injuries. I called at the home, again as the professional Christian wearing the dog collar, into a situation in which it was hard to find God. The emptiness, the devastation, the anger, the reality and the awfulness of human suffering were creating many questions in my mind. The clichéd phrases were so awfully hollow and offensive to the pain. 'It was God's will.' 'You will get over the pain.' 'There is one more angel in heaven.' 'God must have loved her a lot to take her so young.' How often has the real pain of people been trivialised? What kind of God do some of these comments portray?

Faith at times has not been allowed to question or to doubt. There are times when I believe we need to be more honest and allow people and ourselves to be angry with God. To encourage questions and affirm doubts. Religious clichés can sometimes bind people into accepting that which is unacceptable. Suffering really does stink. It is awful. There are times on this earth when many people have to face what appears to be hell itself. We cannot sanitise it, we cannot take it away and we most certainly cannot explain it.

These are only two examples of the extremities of pastoral care and they both came in my first year of ordained ministry. I have experienced many other moments since and some of them are still too raw for those involved, including myself, to mention. I was so sure of my theology when I was ordained, my explanations for suffering were neat and tidy, but the answers did not fit the reality. From my own evangelical background which had not encouraged me to question and doubt, these issues caused ripples in my faith journey. They made me question so much. There is randomness to suffering and grief. It does not make sense. However, I now believe that God has not said that it will. In my own reflection it became clearer to me that the problem was not God but some of the theological constructs that I had accepted. I had accepted a faith were everything was black and white. I had accepted a faith that had all the answers to the hard questions. The pastoral struggle still takes a toll on my vocation and faith. I still struggle with the questions and I still find these moments excruciating. In fact they are probably more difficult, because I am in my present parish for nearly eleven years and I know and love so many of the people who are facing suffering. However, I have stopped trying to explain or understand the mystery of suffering. It does not make sense and all I can do, as I believe in the incarnation, is to try and help people find something of his promise, 'I am with you.'

Alongside these questions was the fact that my ordination took place at the height of what we now call 'The Troubles'. We were and still are a very divided community. In this situation the collar in some people's minds automatically aligned you with one side. I was a Protestant cleric and I was therefore ministering to and for that community. Our country had become more polarised and I was part of that. This is not something I sought but it came with the territory.

Within my first few years of ministry something of this struggle became more apparent to me again through the anvil of suffering. I found myself taking part in the funeral of a young RUC constable who had been murdered by an IRA bomb. I had met him and his fiancé as they prepared for their wedding. A few weeks before their wedding day, we were singing the hymns that should have been sung at their wedding. The television cameras, the radio microphones, the journalists and the whole media circus were present. The politicians made their way past the cameras to make sure they were seen. Statements were issued and interviews were recorded. In the middle of this was the most awful human tragedy. The waste, the pain, the grief, and what could this possibly achieve? The dreadful sin of murder caused anger and resentment. Mingled with many emotions was the question, 'What is the ministry of the church in this situation?' To some people our involvement was politicising this awful event and yet we had to be there and wanted to be there, especially for the bereaved. The trappings of media and political issues I believe made it much harder for a family to grieve. It was all so public. This pain was brought about by somebody simply doing his job and others took his life because of his uniform.

Part of the difficulty in ministering in this divided community is that people have expectations of you. They assume you will behave in certain ways, they can even demand that you do. You will let the side down if you do not do as expected. This could often be seen in the context of ecumenical relationships. This is the concept of developing relationships with other churches, although in Northern Ireland the controversy is about relationships with the Roman Catholic Church if you are a Protestant. My university days in Belfast and Dublin had stretched my own thinking on this subject. I am forever grateful to my mum for teaching me not to judge or exclude people because of where they worshipped or because of what they religion they were. I was even before my ordination committed to building bridges with other Christians. It was instinctive to me.

There are those inside and outside the church who are dia-
metrically opposed to building any relationships with the
Catholic Church in our community. For some it is because of
religious conviction and it is therefore a no-go area. They are also
very unhappy with anyone from their tradition who seeks to go
there. This is a logical position – if it is wrong for them then it is always wrong. I suppose from that perspective what is even worse
is when people try to lead others on an ecumenical journey.

One of the funniest moments I experienced in this part of my
ministry was when I met the new parish priest in Ardglass. He
had arrived in the parochial house and I called to welcome him.
He introduced himself by saying: 'If you are from the Malone
Road you will call me William, if you are from the Shankill Road
you will call me Billy and if you are from the Falls Road you will
call me Liam.' We became good friends and he really liked to be
called Liam. He was a delightful character and was coming near
the end of his ministry. He had experienced things in his ministry in West Belfast that I could not even begin to imagine. We
worked hard together at visiting homes of a few couples who
were seeking inter-church marriages. We would walk through
the village together and were genuine friends. My mum even
knit him an Aran cardigan and he wore it with great pride, especially because a 'Prod' knit it.

However, before Father Liam arrived the previous parish
priest had died. As a fellow human being I attended his funeral
Mass and was welcomed warmly by bishop, priests and people.
I discovered by a few anonymous phone calls that this had upset
some people. I do believe that these were not from any parishioners. This was not a major event but it highlights for me how I
was expected to behave as a Protestant minister in the minds of
some people. There are times when I have felt pressure to do
things and behave in certain ways that I am not happy with. I
have always sought to be true to myself but I am sure I have
been a coward and have justified myself by calling it expediency.
To be a disciple of Jesus in such a religious and political culture
is actually a real struggle for those who try to act with integrity
and to have a prophetic voice.

My struggle with ordination in these early years was immense. So many issues came to the fore. So many questions were
being posed. So many expectations appeared to be making demands on what I should do and be. I was also struggling with
being the professional Christian who had to say his prayers and
find a deepening of spiritual life. Of course I was meant to be
doing the same for others as well. I was also living in a different
home and community and adjusting to local cultures and expectations. A myriad of thoughts and issues were racing and there
was little structure or support where these issues could be addressed except for the friends that I had been in college with. As
in theological college, there was still the danger, I thought, that I
was being asked to conform, to do things in a certain way and
definitely not to ask the difficult questions.

Within the religious culture there was the easy and trite
answer: 'Just pray.' Others might just tell me to get on with
preaching the gospel. There might be those who would think the
problems were within myself and of my own making. What I
was seeking to do was to discover myself in this vocation. I believed then, and still do, that the greatest gift I bring to this vocation is the gift of myself. I found that I could not be what some
others wanted me to be, whether that is from a theological perspective, a political perspective or from those who expected the
minister to do everything.

In the religious culture of this beautiful place it is easy to find
the life of faith being about rules and regulations. My journey of
faith has been more cluttered than it should have been. Within
my own spirit I want to know and love Jesus more than anything else. The religious community can make that more difficult
because it can have such a narrow focus on what that actually en-
tails. I suppose I had seen this earlier in my life with my mum's
experience.

It was the religious people in his day who made Jesus' life
difficult. This religiosity, as have experienced it, is always right
and self-righteous. It is always quick to find fault in others. It always seems to have answers to the impossible questions. There

is no room for doubts or questioning, only an absolute conviction in the life hereafter and that is all that matters. This is probably a caricature, but it is how I have felt at times.

These issues are still part of my vocation now. They are part of what I will always wrestle with as I seek to follow the call I believe I have. Writing about these struggles has helped me to clarify them and, despite them, I am still able to move forward on my journey. I hope it will also help many others who, in this beautiful place, are seeking to follow Jesus, whether ordained or not. I will return to the areas that have helped me on this journey that gives fulfilment and frustration.

CHAPTER 4

Expectations

It was strange being addressed as 'Reverend Abernethy'. I was ordained and I had taken my ordination vows. My future now was to be a minister of the church, at this stage a deacon. Yet within me was the desire to be treated the same. I had not changed. I was essentially the same person. My personality had not changed. My role and function were different but I did not want people to treat me differently, especially those who had always known me. Somewhere within me was the struggle with the fact that I had crossed an imaginary line and I was now part of the system and establishment.

Ordination did not just bring a different form of being addressed and of dress. It also brought a new role, a new function and a whole new way of life. There was no job description and no job contract. There appeared to be many assumptions that I should and would know what to do. I was left to get on with the job as instructed by my rector. Talking to my friends who had also been recently ordained, they were experiencing the same expectations.

It would be difficult to write a job description, as the clause 'anything else deemed necessary' would have to be included, to allow for the many things that just kept appearing. The job description would also vary depending on which member of the parish you asked to formulate it. As John Sandford writes: 'Perhaps in no other profession is a person facing so many expectations from so many people and, to make the situation more complicated, the expectations people place upon the minister vary enormously … some people expect their priest or minister to be a great teacher, others want him foremost to be a faithful pastor, others hand him the task of being a financial wizard, some want him to maintain the old traditions, but just as many want him to be pleasingly avant garde (yet not threaten them too much!) Some expect him to devote himself to calling on the sick, or making parish calls, or attending community social functions, or being concerned with the poor or civil rights, while others want him for a personal counsellor ... Furthermore these people with their expectations are persons who must be reckoned with. These are the ones who pay the bills.' (*Ministry Burnout*, J. A. Sanford, pages 7-8.)

I distinctly remember feeling bewildered by the many things I was expected to do. It would be easy to criticise the training, but the job I was now doing could only be prepared for by doing it. There was a constant pace of doing things that at times was relentless. There was also the frustration of rarely being able to finish anything. The sudden shift in emotions was also strange. Moving from birth to death in the space of minutes. The problem that I found most difficult was saying my prayers because I had to rather than because I wanted to. In the middle of all this there was the need to write a sermon or a talk for assembly or the Bible study group. Then of course there was time for family, friends and myself. The training I received could not have prepared me for this. Perhaps being trained as I tried to do the job would have been a better model, a subject I will return to in a later chapter.

The trust that was given to me was staggering and it still is. People would tell me their life stories, their hopes, their fears, and trust with me with personal and private matters. It needs to be stated that this trust is something that I value immensely and I never tell anyone what is told to me in these circumstances, not even Liz, my wife. In her own profession as a medical doctor she lives by the same rule. I also find it amazing to be allowed immediate entry into so many homes. There is often that feeling of my presence being valued and of ministry being appreciated. Undoubtedly there might be the occasional difficult moment but these are rare. Of course in the early years I was given a 'fool's pardon' because I was the young curate. People seemed to take great delight in feeling they were part of shaping my ministry for the future.

In the midst of the busy schedule I was very conscious of spending a lot of time reacting to people and situations. The day could have been planned beautifully but something happened that demanded immediate attention. This is a principle that has been evident in every phase of ministry; in fact it is all the more the case now, as I have spent longer in my present parish than ever before. The need to be available for people is fundamental if pastoral care is to have any integrity. There may be times when this is difficult for genuine reasons, but availability is a priority. There may also be times when certain people need to be given parameters for that availability if they become too demanding.

No matter what meeting I found myself at or whatever parish group I visited, my opinions and my thoughts were expected. I was never just *at* a meeting, but wherever I went I was there as the minister and not as a private individual. The function carried with it certain expectations. I was the minister and therefore was expected to have answers, or to have new ideas, or to be able to recruit new leaders or members for any and every organisation. Above all I felt I was meant to give some kind of official blessing or approval to whatever was happening. I wanted to be with people as an individual but that proved impossible. I would find myself having to take some kind of leadership role. One of the dangers I discovered in this is that I was being used, at times, to try to further somebody else's agenda.

It was and is strange being in situations where my presence is more about my function as a minister than about whom I am as a person. The tension of wanting to be just another member of the group or committee or leadership team is still part of the struggle of ordination. The wearing of the collar and the title means that in every situation there is the expectation that I will be in charge or be setting the agenda. Even those who resent this still expect it to be the case, and thereby I become a target for them to express their discontent and frustration. Some of the most difficult people in this situation are the religious people who appear to have no difficulty knowing what God wants to do, whereas I am not so sure. Maybe this says more about my faith that always questions and doubts – a faith that finds itself more at home in contemplation and reflection than in decisive action.

The model of ministry that I inherited was given to me indirectly. Nobody ever explained it. I arrived at ordination and the assumption seemed to be that I and other clergy were the ministry. Everyone else was a recipient. The separation between clergy and laity in the model and structure I was ordained into was very stark. There are signs of change in the church but the process is long and arduous.

Edward Schillebeeckx writes: 'I am not against the institutions of the church. But they are human historical institutions which had to evolve for the good of Christians … The institutions are based on the fact that there is a church, but the institution as such is a human institution … They are an evolution … I believe it has to change.' (*I am a Happy Theologian*, Edward Schillebeeckx, page 72.) The model of ministry that I inherited appears to stand starkly against the heart of ministry as expressed in the New Testament. St Paul describes 'the body of Christ' where every member has a role, a function, a God-given gift to exercise for the good of the whole. We state as a church that we believe in the priesthood of all believers. We do argue in the Church of Ireland whether people become believers in this sense at baptism or conversion, but whichever we believe everyone has a ministry. This separation between clergy and laity has caused great stress in ministry. It has caused great frustration among the laity. It has been discussed for decades. The first person I heard take this subject seriously was the late Canon David Watson. He was a man who had great vision and wonderful gifts of communication. He sought to model a ministry which included everyone, lay and ordained, in St Michael-le-Belfry in York. Liz and I visited this place with two friends, Roy and Audrey, in 1985 and were inspired by the reality of what was happening. There were arguments, differences of opinion and resistance to change but they were moving forward as a team of people trying to make real ministry for all.

There are good reasons why developing new models is difficult. There is a whole process of re-education needed for clergy and people. There are people who, through genuine diffidence, feel they are unworthy to do anything. There are others who are unhappy to do anything in case they are seen as pushing themselves forward. There is a concern at times as to how other people in the parish might react. Clergy may feel people will think they are shirking their job. There are those who apparently think clergy only work one day a week. If only that were true! There are probably many people who would love to help but who have never been asked. I also believe collaborative ministry can be threatening to clergy, as they will have to share themselves with others and be vulnerable. They will have to learn to trust and be open to affirmation and criticism. I can also say that developing this kind of ministry takes planning, training and preparing a parish for change, and that will take a long time if the changes are to be lasting. The people of Ballyholme are preparing themselves for more change when 'yer man' has been away thinking, praying and writing. However, in all of this I also believe that this style of ministry is a less lonely road to travel.

Recently I discussed my job description with a support group of lay people in Ballyholme. These are people who have helped formulate our recent parish strategy for the next five years. They felt the essentials of my task are: preaching, handling pastoral crises (especially bereavement) and leading worship. The latter of these was to include all the occasional offices, which are baptism, weddings and funerals. These were to be the main focus in allotting my time and energy. I found this a helpful process. Although I would have to add that one of my concerns as we did this was that there was no time for forward planning and training of others. It was good to share my struggle with the job and to be affirmed in what I feel called to do. Obviously there are many things I have to do but these discussions helped me map out possible ways of sharing the ministry of the church with others. I think it also empowered those who so often feel excluded from the life of the church to have an input and to hear my own struggles. There is a journey ahead that will be interesting, and probably slower than I would like it to be, but it helps to know that I am not alone as we journey. It helps us ask questions about how we can equip others for the work of the ministry rather than try to do the impossible and fail. I believe resentment, frustration and cynicism come from many clergy feeling isolated, alone, misunderstood, taken for granted and not receiving any affirmation. I have heard it said that parishes end up with the clergy they deserve. It is good for people other than clergy to share in the leadership of the church; there are insights from the pew that we have found invaluable. This journey for us has only begun but it is a journey the ministry must travel if it is to be reclaimed by those to whom it has been given, the body of Christ, God's people.

The future strategy must allow for this direction. Issues such as re-educating, training, delegating, developing leadership structures and others must be addressed. This will take time and I trust, as I see other parishes already ahead of us on this journey, that we can share experiences and lessons together.

It is obvious over the centuries that different patterns of ministry have evolved and the handing on of apostolic authority became a major issue to be addressed. Leaders were seen as a focus for unity and authenticity. This was best expressed in the Eucharist. This is not the place for a detailed analysis of church history but the role of the clergy, the theology of ordination and the essence of ministry have become major issues for the church today. There is an enormous amount of material written on these subjects. I believe clericalism has become an issue for the church and especially in our highly religious culture. This is a problem that has become more difficult as clergy have at times become the brunt of jokes. Very often in television programmes clergy are presented as weak and confused. They are either very fundamentalist or ridiculously liberal. All this affects the problem we want to address. How do we re-write the script for the clergy? Ministry is for all and those who are ordained have a special role and function. However, their ministry is validated and truly productive if they are affirmed and respected by those to whom and with whom they minister. Clergy, as I see this, only have a function within a local community that recognises their ministry and gifts and is willing to share that ministry with them. We are the people of God who minister to one another and to those who find faith difficult or impossible. We are there in the fellowship of Christ's church to serve one another and those who do not belong, no matter who they are or what they believe.

I am conscious that in what I have said I have deliberately avoided a discussion of the theology of ordination or priesthood. Within my own denomination there are those who hold strong and very different views on this subject. These views do divide and cause pain for people. I think that in what I am trying to argue a discussion on the theology of ordination is not essential. Whatever our view of ordination and priesthood, we cannot avoid the question of what is our view of the ministry of all God's people. Whether we have a high or low view of ordination, the body of Christ gives to all who are members an identity, a calling and gifts to offer for the good of all.

In all of this there is a process of re-education. Many people in the pew still want things to be as they have been. Change is always a difficult thing to handle. They want to be the recipients rather than participants. I find Alistair Redfern's reflections on this very helpful. 'The industrial revolution produced a culture of voluntary consumers, and this became the mark of the church. Now the *mono minister* became ... the tent pole that bore the increasing weight of maintaining the church as an institution in a hostile and uncertain world. There are many offers of assistance, but in a professional culture all these lay contributions must be arranged and controlled by a trained public minister. They became the tent poles who are increasingly buckling under the weight of expectations which were associated with previous images but are unrealistic in the modern world.'(*Ministry and Priesthood,* Alistair Redfern, page 45.)

For the good of everyone we have to find new models and forms of ministry in the parish base. It is my belief that we need to do this in different contexts. As different parishes encourage the ministry of God's people, the lessons can be shared and we can help each other on our respective journeys.

After twenty years in ordained ministry, I believe this is the most critical issue that needs to be addressed by the church. I know of clergy who have left parish ministry because of the sheer frustration of not being allowed to minister in any way but this old model. I know of many people who sit in the pew who have left their parish church because they were not given a ministry. I know of clergy who have become damaged by carrying this burden on their own. The expectations of people in church life have clashed with their vision of ministry and they have not been able to stay in parish ministry. There are clergy who are uncertain how to move this process forward. I find myself longing to travel this road but uncertain how to do it. I am very thankful for a parish that have been patient with me as I have shared my struggle. As I continue to try to share the ministry with more people I know there will be tensions and growing pains. When delegation takes place people can feel threatened, trust can be abused and private agendas can be pursued. However, under God we must take risks with ministry. This will help those who are ordained to find affirmation and support. It will also help many others not ordained to receive the opportunity and privilege of being channels of God's peace and presence. We must be an incarnational church working out how we together can make a difference in a world that has so much loneliness and pain. In the process we will all find our own journey of faith bringing growth and fulfilment.

Steven Croft sums up the situation very clearly: 'The models of mission and ministry that have sustained the church through previous centuries are no longer proving effective or sustainable for the majority of congregations and of clergy.' (*Ministry in Three Dimensions*, Steven Croft, page 4.)

With fewer clergy, and more clergy suffering from stress and even leaving the ordained ministry, and the church generally in decline, we will have to be prepared to do things differently for the good of all. However, I do find this exciting because I believe that every problem is an opportunity. The greatest gift God has given us is the gift of faith and after that it is the gift of each other. With those amazing assets I look forward to the journey ahead with him.

CHAPTER 5

The Paradox

My own life experiences have always been a constant touch-stone for my faith and vocation. They give me insights into the ups and downs of being human. I believe they help me as I seek to bring empathy and compassion to others. They also help me as I face the tensions of theology and experience, of making faith more than just pious words or hollow clichés. At the heart of my struggle has been paradox. I return to one very profound experience as a window into this struggle.

The phone rang very late one Tuesday evening in January 2000. The voice was very distressed and for her to ring for help it must be serious. I arrived at the same time as the ambulance. She was admitted to the Royal Victoria Hospital, Belfast. I left her in the early hours of the Wednesday morning and she was making a good recovery from a mild stroke. The following Sunday morning the phone rang at about three o'clock in the early hours. The sister from the ward told me to come quickly, my mum had had a much more serious stroke. The next nineteen days were spent watching, hoping and despairing. My brother came from Canada, and my auntie Dora and uncle Ivor were a constant support. Nearly three weeks later, in the early hours of a Friday morning, death came to her as a friend.

I sat with her for a while and I prayed with her. In theological terms some might worry that I was praying for the dead. I was simply giving her back to God. I was praying that she at last would find complete healing and peace from the pain that life had at times given her. I knew she was now at peace in the love that had helped her through some very difficult and dark days. I was giving thanks that, for her, death was not the end. Through my tears I was letting go of someone who had given me so much. It was only as she lay in hospital that I was able to tell her, without the usual embarrassment, of how much I loved her. Any show of emotion or affection was very difficult with my mum. Her natural reserve and her life experience meant she did not divulge her feelings with hugs and kisses. She was not at all demonstrative. Her love was shown by always being there, in hoping for the best and in her endless acts of kindness. I found an amazing paradox in my mum's death. I was sore and I was now an orphan but I was so relieved that her struggle was over and she was at peace.

The sorrow and the relief of my mum's death have been a comfort to me since. As I reflect upon the special moments of my life, there always appears to be a paradox.

When my dad left us when I was six, I was to discover the most amazing relationship with my 'poppy', my grandfather's family name. When Liz and I were to get married I was terrified of the commitment but thrilled at finding someone who loved me so unconditionally. When our two children were born, Peter and Ruth, there was the unmistakeable 'wow' of awe and wonder at the miracle of birth. There was also the huge responsibility that lay ahead of being a parent.

There are so many paradoxes in our lives and paradoxes are very much part of being human. We can find so many in the biblical revelation. Out of the void and emptiness God created the world and all that is in it. The Book of Genesis does not deal with how in any scientific way but it does highlight the origin of what I believe to be a miracle. Throughout the Old Testament God makes covenants with his people and they constantly break them. There is the paradox of a great deal of bloodshed and death amidst the growing revelation of a love-struck God seeking to bring his creation back to himself.

There is the incredible paradox of God coming into the world as a tiny helpless baby. I can never accept the idea presented in the Christmas carol: 'no crying he makes'. All babies cry and I am sure this one was no exception. This gift was eventually rejected and killed even though he was innocent of any crime. Then we have the ultimate statement of faith: this man died and rose again. He appeared to many and from a frightened hapless group of disciples allowed his ministry to continue through them. This church still exists today despite many mistakes and dreadful crimes committed in its name.

Paradox is at the very heart of faith. It is at the heart of human existence. We can create the most amazing inventions as we fly people to the moon. We can fly around the world. We can save lives by various transplants and very sophisticated medicines and medical machinery. Yet at the same time we sell instruments of mass destruction and leave millions dying of starvation. We give millions to charities and worthy causes and yet there are many living on the streets and in poverty. We in this beautiful country are renowned for being religious and devout and yet we can hide behind religious labels and have killed each other with ease. For those who have not killed there are many who refuse to listen to one another, or who judge one another because of religious affiliation.

I see it within myself. I am generally a reasonable, rational and caring person but behind the wheel of a car I find everyone else has horns. My children will be the first to verify this part of me; in fact they are helping me to learn to laugh at myself, or maybe I have no choice. Children are a real gift – they have helped me not take myself too seriously.

Paradox is at the centre of personal faith as well. My own faith journey has been one of doubts, questions and struggles. Yet it has also been one of amazing moments of insight, belief and wonder. There are times when I am concerned that faith is presented as a mathematical equation. If you add faith and trust you have a perfect salvation. Faith is a gift I have been given. Trust is something that takes time to grow and it will be challenged. The doubts and questions need to be recognised and reflected upon. Kenneth Leech's comments are important on this subject: 'Hence the tragic, but all too common phenomenon of the Christian believer, whether of catholic or evangelical variety, who protects himself or herself from any real critique or threat by an acquired jargon. Certainties and pious clichés are repeated parrot-fashion, real dialogue becomes impossible, and conflict and questioning are systematically repressed.' (*True God*, Kenneth Leech, page 25.)

As I reflect upon the disciples after the resurrection, they were confused, doubting and bewildered. Slowly but surely they moved forward. The New Testament is also written to people who were struggling with faith and needed to be encouraged. I need this help from others on the journey. I find Phillip Yancey's observation very helpful: 'God's invisibility guarantees I will experience times of doubt.' (*Searching for the Invisible God*, Phillip Yancey, page 37.)

Recently someone wrote to me and I quote a few lines from their letter, which I found very encouraging: 'Your principle of faith without doubt being no more than blind obedience helped me resolve a number of issues from my upbringing. There is still a long way to go but I'm looking forward to the journey.'

I have never doubted the existence of God. I have questioned how this amazing creator God can allow such pain and hell to be part of the human experience. For others there will be different questions and struggles. I am concerned that many people have been made to doubt their own faith because they are made to feel guilty for having doubts. I certainly cannot explain why some people have more than their fair share of suffering. I cannot explain why some people die so tragically. I cannot comprehend why some people of faith talk of love but cannot make peace with other people of faith.

The Easter faith of death and resurrection helps me believe that, as I struggle with my questions and doubts, my faith dies and bursts into new life again. My faith grows and is nurtured by facing this struggle in the midst of a world where faith in God can be difficult. However, as that faith is discovered and experienced it can grow and mature into a faith that can use doubts and questions to bring depth and strength. 'But true faith can only grow and mature if it includes the elements of paradox and creative doubt ... Without such creative doubt, religion becomes hard and cruel, degenerating into spurious security which breeds intolerance and persecution.'(*True God*, Kenneth Leech, page 25.)

The faith I was given and have found growing is not about believing a list of concepts but about a personal relationship with a friend whom I have questioned, been angry with and yet have come to depend on so much. This relationship is based on love that I have found, giving me security and strength as I seek to live out my vocation.

The same paradox is at the heart of my vocation. The frustrations, the difficulties must be faced, addressed and worked through to find the fulfilment that comes as a gift. The fulfilment I have found in ministry has often come paradoxically from the people who have been in terrible pain. I feel I have done nothing except be there and yet the affirmation and encouragement I have received has been fulfilling. This fulfilment did not come without the frustration of finding the emotional demands very great. This fulfilment comes after I have been angry with God for the pain others have to face. This fulfilment comes as the busyness of ministry makes me resent the constant demands and needs of others.

I cannot and will not find the fulfilment that I need in ministry without being available to others and without having to work within church structures that have not addressed the many changes that have taken place within our society and culture. I need to learn ways of coping with the frustrations and of changing what I can. As I do so I am more likely to find the fulfilment of serving God and others in this vocation. There is a terrible danger in my experience that at times I have wanted the fulfilment of ministry without the frustration. We cannot experience the wonderful joy of Easter Day without recognising the pain and emptiness of Good Friday.

I want to remember the paradox of my mum's death, as even in her death she speaks to me about how I can continue to develop and live with my vocation. This is a vocation that she helped develop. At the heart of that same vocation is a faith that I will continue to struggle with. It is in my questioning and my doubts that my faith will be able to grow. Thanks be to God for his gifts of paradox and faith.

CHAPTER 6

The Job of Caring

There have been times when I have found myself emotionally and spiritually exhausted. I have felt numb, angry, confused and not wanting to be with people. I want to withdraw from all social contact and find ways of making sense of the emptiness. Pastoral ministry is enormously demanding. To spend every day with people who are in pain of illness or bereavement, with people who are unable to make sense of life, with people who have been hurt and are angry – all these and other situations leave me drained. Often the very act of being with people in their pain and struggle takes away my energy and strength.

A few years ago after a very demanding period of sickness and death I wakened in the middle of the night feeling unwell and with pains in my arms. Quickly I found myself in the coronary care unit of the local hospital. I hadn't even had my fortieth birthday. For my family and me this was a sudden shock. They did not like the sight of me wired up to various monitors. Liz was her usual supportive and reassuring presence but I knew she was still anxious.

Eventually I was released from hospital. I had been on the treadmill for nineteen minutes and complained that my legs were sore. My consultant was very helpful and assured me there was nothing wrong except exhaustion. I was ordered to rest and to take time to recover from the emotionally and physically draining job of caring.

It is important not to suggest that ministry was the reason I ended up in hospital. My personality, my inability to say no, my difficulty in relaxing and my desire to do all I could were part of the problem. However, I do know the exhaustion was weariness with sadness. When I was starting to resent people dying, when my stomach churned when the phone rang, I knew I was losing the ability to care. I was losing my compassion.

I spent much time reflecting on this moment, especially during the time I was told to take off work. The people around me were wonderfully supportive and the select vestry and people of Ballyholme were very affirming. During this time I resigned from many committees. I had to ask some difficult questions and examine again what it was I was called to do. Other people in different jobs have had to do the same. In discussion with other people in the caring professions, I certainly came to the conclusion that it was the emotional turmoil of sickness and dying that made me feel so empty.

Over a period of more than ten years I have conducted more than four hundred funerals. There are other clergy who have borne the heat and burden of the day with more than that. I cannot comment on how others survive.

For myself, I knew I had to look at how I was going to survive if I was to offer care to those who needed support. I am not sure I have found the answer to how I can cope with the relentless pain that so many have to face. 'The other area in which ministers of religion are notoriously bad at caring for themselves is in their response to a "received" dictum of total availability and a merging of personal and professional such as would not be tolerated by many other people.' (*Clergy Stress*, Mary Anne Coate, page 94.)

There might be those who would suggest I should not get so emotionally involved with people, but withhold some of myself and just stand alongside people. I am not that kind of person. I feel things very deeply. I am sensitive to pain and hurt. No doubt I am sensitised by my childhood experience. There are serious questions surrounding this ministry of care. What is the role of the minister? What is the role of the church in this situation? My vocation has at its heart a call to be with the sick, those in pain and especially the bereaved. It is at these moments that yet again the paradox of ministry is evident. The danger of giving and yet the fulfilment it brings. To be able to bring comfort to those in pain is an amazing privilege, especially when representing the one who is the source of all comfort.

The tension is something I am learning to live with. I cannot but be vulnerable to the pain of others. However, I also need to learn to get help from others, to build support structures and escape routes if I find my compassion being drained from my spirit. I want to return to this in a later chapter because these supports are not just for the job of caring but for all aspects of keeping vocation alive in the midst of the frustrations and tensions that ministry in the church brings.

Over the years of ministering to the bereaved there are many issues that have caused me concern. I believe that this area of pastoral care is one of the most demanding and yet important that we are involved in. In our culture death is a subject that many of us find difficult to address. 'We rarely understand how to treat our own sorrows or those of others.' (*Framley Parsonage,* Anthony Trollope, page 141.)

Grief is a very difficult emotion. Facing death and the death of a loved one is an emotional roller coaster. There is no medicine that can ease the pain and there are no words that can make it better. It is a journey people have to make and yet there is no end to this journey. One of the greatest myths about bereavement is that people are told, 'You will get over it.' This denies the awful finality of death. We will never see our loved one again. The gap they leave in our lives is irreplaceable. There are those who can say they have learned to live with the pain, they can finds ways of coping. However, for some the pain is so deep they can never find the same joy and purpose in living. Many of these people can be made to feel very isolated and alone because others do not understand. They can be made to feel they don't have faith or that their faith is not strong enough.

I have become convinced that everybody copes with bereavement differently and everybody needs to be allowed the space to do this. I have been impressed with many groups working within the community, especially those nursing cancer patients; they give such wonderful support to the sick and their relatives along this journey of facing the inevitable and beyond.

This journey of grief is, I believe, the most difficult and profound journey any of us make. For those who have faith, the journey is not necessarily easier. There are so many questions, doubts and issues that leave faith shaken and tested. I do not mean that God deliberately picks on certain people and thereby makes them suffer just to see if they can prove the depth of their faith. Often I have heard people say, 'It must be God's will', 'The Lord wanted them for himself', and I cringe. I find these sentiments offensive to grief and an outrage against God. It does not allow for the randomness and the awfulness of suffering. The struggle with grief can be made so much more difficult for people if they have to cope with the thought that God did this deliberately to test them.

C. S. Lewis, in his book *A Grief Observed*, makes some telling comments: 'Because she is in God's hands. But if so, she was in God's hands all the time, and I have seen what they did to her here. Do they suddenly become gentler to us the moment we are out of the body? And if so why?' (page 24.) There is a danger that in our religious culture we have crushed or avoided the difficult questions. There can be an attempt to give simplistic comments to questions that do not have answers. Suffering is a mystery that I cannot explain. We must try and justify things that are unjustifiable. I will never believe that it is God's will that cancer should exist. I will never believe that children are meant to die. There are tragedies in this life that are awful and cannot be rationalised. What I do believe is that God has entered this world, that contains so much of hell, and has been with us in it. It never ceases to amaze me how people in hell itself can find comfort and strength that cannot be explained. For those who find their hell overwhelming, it is not necessarily a lack of faith.

We must never make people feel that they are somehow less Christian because they struggle with the enormity of suffering and pain. People need to be given space to ask their questions, to express their doubts and not have their struggle suffocated by religious clichés.

In my experience there are no answers to the difficult questions, only that terrible silence. Again I turn to C. S. Lewis as he reflected on his grief and questions. He has no answers. 'When I lay these questions before God I get no answer. But a rather special sort of "No answer". It is not the locked door. It is more like a silent, certainly not uncompassionate gaze.' (*Grief Observed*, pages 54-55.)

However, I return to the ministry of care when the crisis strikes. How do we minister to the dying and bereaved? Here all I can do is share some of my experience in seeking to do this. Part of the difficulty in the larger parishes is that there may be homes to which we are called where we do not know the family and the connection with the parish is very tenuous. There may be those who want to argue that this is not our role and we shouldn't be there as we are just being used. In my moments of tiredness and weariness of spirit I can empathise with this view. Yet I cannot leave people at such a vulnerable moment thinking the church didn't care. I cannot stand in judgement on people's lives – I have enough difficulty keeping my own relationship with the Lord alive and well.

I take the basic principle that I will be there for those who are in pain and need. I would love to be able to say that this has led to many converts and new church members but I cannot. I do believe it means that people have been able to experience a compassionate church that does not just talk the talk but tries to walk it. I must confess that my thoughts on this are very subjective and influenced profoundly by my mum's experience of church.

When a family are experiencing the finality of death, what is our role? I am particularly thinking of the ordained minister. There are those who would argue it is our responsibility to declare the gospel in very clear terms. To use this opportunity to make people face the reality that it could be them next. I am unhappy about this because I believe this is an abuse of people's pain. My experience is that families are trying to cope with the many emotions of grief. There is the finality of death. Even when death is expected it is still a shock. There may be guilt of things not said or done. There may be memories of regrets left unresolved. There may be numbness, watching yourself doing things but not being engaged with it. There are the questions that surface about life after death and heaven and hell.

In the trauma of death I believe our responsibility is to help the family gather together their memories, their thankfulness, their pain and their questions, to help them face the questions and to talk about them. Our role is to facilitate them and to be a presence and a support. To enable them to do things they need to do but are finding it difficult to do. The gospel in the process is proclaimed, and the liturgy and scripture, as much as any of our words, can help as well.

Throughout our culture and society we find death difficult. There is a danger in the context of faith that we fail to face the stark finality of death and thereby miss the incredible hope. Death cannot be talked away by religious jargon and it cannot be dissolved as if we were wiping up a mess on the floor. The profound shock, finality and pain of death cannot be made better by saying death is not the end. Yes we have hope, yes we believe in life after death, but for those facing death we must let them face the darkness. As people are allowed the space to doubt and question they can find faith growing. When death happens it is not all right and they will not get over it. They may in time learn to live with pain. God has not promised to remove the pain but to be with us in our pain. We need to help people seek, knock and find for themselves the light in the darkness. We cannot give them easy answers and we cannot switch on the light. We can be with them and enable them to move forward. To do this we will experience our own vulnerability in dealing with pain.

Vulnerability is the ultimate mark of ministry to those in crisis. To be vulnerable with them is part of our calling. To empathise with people and to try and discern their struggle is fundamental to what we must do. It is critical not to condemn or judge or to wish the pain would go away. 'To care about people is not to desire to help them. When we have a desire to help people, then we go out of our way to keep them dependent on us, so we can be helpers. There are too many preachers and teachers who want to help people, to do something for them or to them. There need to be more preachers and teachers who desire only to be with others in ways that make it possible for them to help themselves. Christ did not fall into solution making or problem solving.' (*Spiritual life*, J.Westerhoff, page 31.)

It is in this context that the funeral service, the visiting and the ongoing pastoral care is developed. There are certain things that I have found helpful or certain things that others have found helpful. I offer them as touchstones that might be helpful to others.

Families do need time to talk about their loved one. I find it an amazing privilege to hear families talk about the people they loved and maybe even found infuriating. The funny family stories are inevitable, the achievements and the life story are usually fascinating. It never ceases to amaze me what some people have done in their lifetime. It has been helpful on occasions to ask different members of the family to write down their thoughts. How would they describe their loved one in a few sentences? This can be helpful in forming a thanksgiving for a person's life. This raises the issue of the address at the funeral. Is it purely a presentation of the gospel or an exposition of the hope that is ours in Christ or a thanksgiving for the deceased? I do not think that it is a case of choosing one of these options. However, I do believe that the most important people at the funeral are the bereaved family. They need to find comfort, hope and the presence of the Lord in that act of worship. I believe our responsibility is to gather together the thoughts, the emotions, the struggle and the hope for people to help them move forward on their journey of grief. We can do this more effectively if we have listened to the family and found ourselves empathising with them. We must walk with the bereaved through the valley of the shadow of death to help them find light in their darkness.

It is also important to include children in the family grief. For years children were excluded or ignored. It was thought that they were too young and couldn't understand. I am not sure any of us understand the mystery of death and grief. Children do tend to be more honest, more trusting and more natural at expressing their feelings. It has proved helpful to ask children to draw a picture or write a letter or give a favourite something to place in the coffin. It is important to let them grieve and not to assume it doesn't matter to them. There are some groups that work especially with bereaved children. Treetops is one such group which I have experience of and they can be contacted through the Corrymeela Community.

I have also found a candle burning at the funeral a wonderful symbol of hope. We were given some freestanding candlesticks some years ago in memory of a young man who died of cancer. He had been an acolyte in the Lutheran Church in Canada and candlesticks seemed so appropriate. In our Protestant culture a candle can be seen as a divisive symbol because it is used in another denomination. Yet I believe we need symbolism in our search for God's comfort and presence in our pain. Words can sometimes be hollow while music, symbols and silence can help us so much.

It is also useful for members of the family to be encouraged to leave the house and to get some fresh air. Exercise and fresh air might help them get some sleep. It can also give them time and space to think. There are times when families simply need time to be on their own and sometimes this can be difficult if the house is busy with callers.

In our own grief journey since my mum died we also found it very helpful to buy something to remind us of her. We bought a rather expensive coffee machine. She often treated us to coffee in various coffee shops. We now make espressos, cappuccinos and americanos and remember her with love. Remembering is such an important biblical principle. It helps us learn from the past and it helps us move forward, because he is with us now as he always has been.

Therein lies one of the greatest mysteries of death and remembering – the communion of saints that Anglicans declare every time we say one of the creeds. It is difficult to explain a mystery but I firmly believe that those who showed us how to

live by faith are still with us today because in faith they live forever. Their love, their presence, their prayers are with us always.
Death for them is not the end. In time I have come to believe
very firmly that God does not promise us life without pain but
life in our pain. We do have the ultimate hope that one day all
pain, death and mourning will be gone forever, as expressed in
the penultimate chapter of the Book of Revelation.

In times of grief this is a difficult message to hear but it is the
underlying hope of those who hope in him. We cannot understand the mystery of death and suffering but we can experience
his help and strength with us now. Our responsibility in other
peoples' pain is to be something of his presence and help. This
will not mean having answers but hearing the struggle and
questions. Helping others face their struggle so that they might
just learn to live again. That is the ministry to the bereaved
whether we are ordained or not. As we seek to do this we will
also have to be prepared to face our own pain and be vulnerable
with others, and that is for the next chapter.

CHAPTER 7

Caring for the Carer

In drawing alongside others in their pain, it is critical to recognise and face our own emotional struggle. I can never change my childhood. I must not pretend it didn't happen. It has left an indelible mark upon me that profoundly effects how I deal with situations and people. There are times when I have to recognise that in being with others I have to get help for my own needs. In offering care, we ensure that the carer is receiving help so as not to hide behind the mask of being the expert support rather than the wounded helper. Accepting our own vulnerability and asking for help is one of the greatest challenges of public ministry. There is the danger that we portray the glittering image and not our real humanity. If the incarnation means anything then it is not about doing and solving, it is about being human and real. The essence of that being is to be vulnerable. It is my own vulnerability that I share with you in this chapter.

I know, as I look back on my childhood, that the loss of a parent in my life caused many ripples that took me many years to come to terms with. I cannot change my past but I have had to find ways of understanding how it has affected me. Even more important has been to find how it can be redeemed to make me a more compassionate person now. I believe this is an ongoing process of healing that has a relationship with Jesus as its root. It is a journey I will be travelling for the rest of my life. It is in Jesus that I can make sense of all of the experiences I have had, and knowing he is with me makes the journey possible.

If we are involved in the pastoral care of others we often have to be aware of our own needs and pain. I find that when I am vulnerable to the pain of others I am more aware of my own needs. In being vulnerable to the emotional disturbance in others I can find my own pain being re-visited. Over the years I was aware of this and found a spiritual director very helpful. They helped me focus on my journey of faith and my own life story.

In my journey of faith I have always found it difficult to trust God. I have always worried about tomorrow, especially if things are going well because there was bound to be a nasty shock just around the corner. It is debilitating in ministry to be worrying so much. I have not beaten this weakness but I have found help and healing in admitting it and facing it. As I found myself burying many dads, I would return to my own unresolved grief and unanswered questions that were part of the reason I found it so hard to trust. With help I tried to face some of the unresolved grief. For the purpose of this chapter there are two main things I had to face and they involved both my parents. I wrote a letter to my dad that I simply share with you in the hope it might help others.

Dear Dad,

What I want to say I would prefer to say face to face but I have to recognise that may never be possible. Do you feel guilty? Are you angry or do you just not care? My childhood memories are of you being there as my dad. So I like to think you have often wondered about us and how we did. I imagine I look like you because Colin looks like mum and I do not look like his brother.

I have missed you many times during the past years. When I was playing football, rugby and cricket, other dads where there and I wished you could have been too. Throughout the years mum has never spoken ill of you. You are just not mentioned. There were also times I felt angry with you when there was nobody to teach me to drive and no car to drive anyway.

Strange as it may seem, I would like to meet you and let you know my life has turned out well. God is a very important part of my life and I have found his love bringing me healing and help. I also believe that because of what happened I am more compassionate than I might have been. I am not sure how I feel about you but you would always be welcome in our home. You would enjoy my family, my wife Liz, and your grandchildren, Peter and Ruth.

I am glad to write this letter and maybe some day you will see it. I will always remember you with love and affection because you were a sick man. You will always be my dad. Thanks for being my dad and for being with us even for a short while.

Your son,

Alan.

The second thing I did was to start the process of trying to trace him. This proved very difficult, as it was over twenty years since anyone had known of his whereabouts. However, eventually I found myself sitting in the Public Records Office in London looking through the deaths since the early 1970s, as I knew he was alive then. I could not discuss this with my mum, as it was just too painful for her to talk about. The pain was too deep and it was best left alone. However, for me it was different, I had to know.

My heart was racing, my hands were shaking and I felt distinctly unwell as I found his name among the records. I found myself reading and re-reading the insert before I asked for a copy of his death certificate. My mum died without me ever telling her what I had discovered. To complete the circle I share with you the letter I wrote to him after I discovered he was dead.

Dear Dad,

I feel a huge sense of relief that you are dead. I am not sure how I would have dealt with you being alive. You might not have wanted to meet me. There are probably some things better left unsaid.

It is fascinating that you died after I was ordained and after I got married. Did you know? Did you care? Perhaps I am better not knowing. Anyway, what ever happened to you in this life I hope you were at peace at the end. You were obviously ill for some time dying of cancer. I trust you had time to reflect and find light and hope in the darkness.

Through all that happened I believe that I am an OK person. I have found a love in my life that enables me to doubt, to be angry, and it never lets me go. I am still learning to trust that love. This love helps me not to judge others and it also helps me to have compassion for others.

Some day all my questions will be answered, or else the questions won't matter any more. Thanks for being part of who I am and what I am yet to be in him.

Your son,

Alan.

As a child I had found it very difficult to really express what I was feeling. Emotions were difficult to express and for years it had been hard to tell my mum how much she was valued and loved. She would always be awkward if affirmation and love was offered. To help me express how I felt an unusual suggestion was made and it proved invaluable. I wrote her a letter in the form of a tribute I was going to use at her funeral. The following is what I wrote and I gave it to her to read, explaining it was a tribute for her funeral. We had managed to discuss her funeral arrangements before this and she had agreed that I could speak at her funeral. I gave this to her in an envelope and it was returned a few days later with a 'thanks' and an obvious unwillingness to discuss it any further.

Dear Mum,

It is never easy to express emotions and especially to attempt to express love for someone in words. So often they can sound trite, cheap, soppy or insincere. However, words are all we have and perhaps the mistake is that they are often said when they cannot be acknowledged. Please note I did not say 'could no longer be heard' but rather 'no longer acknowledged'. We must state clearly and without hesitation that we believe, and you believed, in the communion of saints and the life everlasting.

You were a woman of few words, of hidden emotions but you always had a very giving and generous heart. Only you know the amount you did for others but I know how much you did for Colin and me. You never broke your promise to us even if you had to do without. You hated lies and loved the truth. You were only really angry at lies and deceit, and we know the truth is the better and more excellent way.

You taught us the value of money and how we were to be generous even with our little. If we were we would always find we would be more than just all right. You taught us to work hard and to give of our best and at all times to enjoy life. Fun and laughter had to be an important part of living because it made the sadness and the pain much easier to cope with. Through your own pain, you always managed to find the good, the positive and the hope that helped keep you going. That strong deep faith, just like poppy's, that was at the core of your being. You, like him, never had to talk about God; you knew that God had been with you and that you had your prayers answered. You found wisdom, strength and peace in your deep faith. There you found strength to keep going, to believe and to keep giving.

My picture of a loving, generous God, who is with us in the ups and downs, I learned from you. Learned not by what you said but by how you lived. Thank God for you and for your faith in him.

You had managed through your experiences to have such a positive attitude to life. You never gave up, as you believed things could only get better. However, you did at times find it hard to trust people, they could let you down, they could cause you pain but you managed to forgive. You did not allow the hurt you experienced to make you cynical or bitter. I often wish some people I visit could learn your ability to be positive, to stop wallowing in self-pity and enjoy what they have been given.

I trust I will always remember that lesson of not to let life make me bitter, unloving and ungrateful.

You did find it hard to allow others to help you, although in later years it was getting easier. Your independence, inner resolve and courage meant it was hard to let others express their love and their care. You always wanted to do it yourself, to be able to look after yourself and never to be a bother. Perhaps that is where I find today difficult because it was hard to tell you, you were loved. You would have been embarrassed and would have reacted awkwardly.

We will never forget the lessons you have left indelibly marked upon our lives. Colin and I say thank you to for all that you gave us. We are proud of you and will be forever grateful for you.

Thanks be to God for you, your faith and your life of love and service.

'Lord, now let your servant go in peace.'

I share these experiences because they have helped me on my journey. I share them because I believe that in being vulnerable with others I have had to face my own pain. Doing so, I think, has made me more able to help others. The cost of pastoral care is immense and we must make sure that we don't become so busy helping others that we do not face our own needs. Vulnerability in caring is costly and part of that cost is being able to ensure we get help for ourselves. That way we are not just the helper but also the one who needs help. We must not get so wrapped up in being the professional that we fail to allow our vulnerability to be strength rather than weakness.

'The person of integrity is first and foremost a critic of self, of tendencies to self-deception and escape from reality, of desire for a false inner security in place of the confrontation with truth which integrity demands.' (*Rediscovering Pastoral Care*, Alistair Campbell, page 12.)

CHAPTER 8

The Gathering

There was no obvious sign of what was to follow. At the time everyone appeared to be smiling and enjoying the moment. I found it a special moment because of how much I enjoy being a dad. From the first day of his life he was full of energy, had no fear and was constantly on the move. It was hard to keep up with him at times.

This particular day we were coming to the end of morning service. The sermon was finished and the offertory hymn was being sung. I have often wondered why the offertory comes after the sermon and should the two be related, in terms of the quality of the sermon? Clergy might get a shock if they were being paid on the basis of the quality of the sermon, never mind the quantity. On this morning in question there were not very many children or young people in the service, which can be quite a common experience in many churches. During the offertory hymn our son decided to go walkabout or, to be more correct, to go and visit dad at the front. Liz was seven months pregnant so she decided to let him go. It would have actually proved very difficult to stop him without facing a showdown. He duly walked up the aisle, up the chancel steps between the choir stalls and up the step into the sanctuary and then wanted to be held in dad's arms. Then he put his head down on my shoulder and smiled. The hymn finished, I gave the blessing and I followed the choir to the rear of the church. My passenger stayed in his place and remained there until his mum took him home.

It was as people were mingling and chatting after the service that I came under a heavy attack. This was done face to face but it was very forceful. Apparently by not sending my son packing

I was 'turning the place into a circus.' This was a genuinely stated belief and a serious criticism of my action. I was shocked, stunned and exhausted. After giving all my energy to lead worship, and after using up all my nervous energy, I was too tired to respond. However, after catching my breath I did suggest that to be asked to choose between her views and rejecting my son, I would be left with no choice. I could find it easy to be dismissive of this view but it is an example of the strength of views that are in church every Sunday. These, and other views surrounding worship, make what happens in worship a very emotive subject.

Some years before this incident, as a young curate I was attempting to bring the young people into the worshipping life of the church. We had carefully planned a 'youth service'; the young people had some excellent ideas regarding this service. The service was not very radical and apart from a few modern songs, young people reading and praying, there was not a great difference from the average evening worship. There was a short drama based on the theme of the service. This was narrated and acted by members of the youth fellowship. It was a simple mime. Everything appeared to be fine until the young people were introduced to do this mime. With a slamming of hymn books and a clicking of the heels, some members of the choir walked down the main aisle and out the back door in protest at the drama. This was all the more effective because of the flowing choir robes. The young people showed amazing grace and wisdom; they waited until the choir members had left the church and then started the drama again. The theme of the drama as it happened was fear and they performed it extremely well.

The protestors waited in the church porch until we were leaving church and then proceeded to tell us how drama was of the devil and we were turning the church into a theatre. These were genuinely held beliefs. I will not dissect them here because I cannot allow a right of reply. I mention this to illustrate again the very strongly held opinions when it comes to worship.

I would want to take issue with how in our religious culture we have always found it easy to express our views but in the process allow no space for differing views. Religious disagreement appears to be about winning the argument rather than allowing healthy discussion and diversity of opinion. For too long in the Protestant tradition in Northern Ireland we are very quick to tell others they are wrong and give them no right to reply. Any attempt to discuss an issue with people who hold very strong views and who do not allow for different views, I have generally found futile. They become so fundamentalist that there is no possibility that they could be wrong or even that a different view might possibly be Christian as well. As I dare to do something different, whether it be with children in church or with drama, the very integrity of my ministry and faith appears to be questioned. In this situation there is little room for compromise or growth. I believe this is one of the great challenges for Christians in Northern Ireland. How can we handle different views without seeking to undermine or question the faith of the person we disagree with?

Let me return to worship and try to focus some thoughts around this subject in the context of parish ministry. The words of N. T. Wright are helpful on this subject:

Worship is humble and glad; worship forgets itself in remembering God; worship celebrates the truth as God's truth, not its own. True worship doesn't put on a show or make a fuss; true worship isn't forced, isn't half-hearted, doesn't keep looking at its watch, doesn't worry what the person in the next pew may be doing. True worship is open to God, adoring God, waiting for God, trusting God even in the dark.

Worship will never end; whether there be buildings, they will crumble; whether there be committees, they will fall asleep; whether there be budgets, they will add up to nothing. For we build for the present age, we discuss for the present age; but when the age to come is here, the present age will be done away. For now we see the beauty of God through a glass darkly, but then face-to-face; now we appreciate only part, but then we shall affirm and appreciate God even as the living God has affirmed and appreciated us. So now our tasks are worship, mission and management, these three; but the greatest of these is worship. (*For all God's Worth*, N. T. Wright, page 9.)

Tom Wright also argues there are two main reasons why we need to focus on this subject. The first is that there are many scripture passages that focus on heaven where worship is the central activity. 'The great multitude in Revelation which no man can number aren't playing cricket. They aren't going shopping. They are worshipping.' He also gives another reason: 'the central task of the church is worship.'(Both quotes from *For all God's Worth*, page 7.)

From the experience of the early followers of Jesus this is obviously the case. In the evolving church history ever since, the church has sought to gather people for worship. Throughout this history there have been various extremes, movements, reactions and experiences that we can reflect upon. For God's people this subject is fundamental. As we worship we discover ourselves 'being invaded by the Shekinah of God.' 'The Shekinah of God being the glory or radiance of God dwelling in the midst of his people. It denotes the immediate Presence of God as opposed to a God who is abstract and aloof.' (Both quotes from *Celebration of Discipline*, Richard Foster, pages 138-9.)

What we do on a Sunday is often described as a service. Worship is more than a collection of hymns, songs, sermons, prayers, Holy Communion or liturgy. These can be a helpful means to an end but in themselves they are not worship. Richard Foster comments that worship happens when 'the Spirit of God touches our human spirit. Forms and rituals do not produce worship, nor the formal disuse of forms and rituals.' The scriptures give us clues as to the various aspects that can go to make up a worship experience, but they do not give a set form. It is critical in any debate about worship within all Christian denominations that the issue does not become a subjective one. How do I prefer worship? What is the way I believe is best suited to real worship? What is it that can be done in our church life to ensure everybody worships the way I want to? These are not the questions we should be asking but unfortunately they have been the reason for so much conflict between God's people over a subject that should bring us together to acknowledge who God is rather than be about our personal preferences or strongly held views.

The worship of God is a community issue, not just for a few. How can we help as many people as possible to experience worship? This will mean different styles of worship being offered rather than one particular style. There is a danger that Christian communities have sought to offer one particular style of worship and yet in every gathering of God's people there will be a very varied gathering of people. This is certainly true in the Church of Ireland parish system. The style on offer may be charismatic, choral, informal, formal, traditional or modern. Not one of these forms guarantees that people will worship; they only offer an avenue for worship. In fact if there is only one style on offer then it is difficult to believe that all are being included in the worshipping community. One particular style that often reflects the rector's preference, in my tradition, will probably exclude others from feeling part of the worshipping community. It appears to be difficult in our culture to allow for diversity and flexibility. We need to seek to be inclusive rather than exclusive. So often in religious communities people can feel excluded because their needs are not being met. Too often Christian groups attract like-minded people instead of being an example to the world of how difference can be handled creatively.

Much of the New Testament epistles are about conflict and difference within the church. There were times when the Christian community had to learn to disagree. The Council of Jerusalem, as recorded in Acts chapter 15, was an attempt to handle difference of opinion. In the fellowship of the church we must be very careful not to be so fixed in our views that we do not allow difference that can enrich us all. As worship is such an important task for the church we need to find ways of handling the conflict that it so often can bring about.

Within our own tradition there have been many divisive

issues on the subject of worship. These are subjects that have caused many an animated argument at synods, in the pages of the *Church of Ireland Gazette*, in many parish churches and homes.

The issue of children in church is one which I have already alluded to earlier in this chapter. I am conscious that there are those who find children an irritant in church. They find 'Family Services' much more like family circuses. Over my time in the ordained ministry I have certainly met people who believe that children should be seen and not heard in church. There are many people of my generation who spent much of a Sunday at church meetings. There was morning Sunday school, followed by a church service and then came afternoon Sunday school. This was a regular diet for many in past decades. I have met people who had such an aversion to an overdose of religion that they find church difficult today. Even when children go to church today they will usually find it a very adult experience. Much of what goes on in churches Sunday by Sunday is a very adult and cerebral experience. There are lots of words and books, little participation, and hymns and songs that are not child friendly.

The introduction of any new hymns or songs can cause consternation to many. To omit any of the liturgy in the Church of Ireland is almost a criminal offence to some. In some churches children are invited to leave church but is that just to get rid of them? I ask the question of our own practice in Ballyholme, as I am not sure how best to handle children in worship. There is in some churches the practice of children's addresses but often the adults enjoy these more than the children. They can be good stories with a moral, rather like a parable and much shorter than sermons.

What do we do to engage our children in worship? Do we give them a sense of joy? Do we give them an experience of belonging? Do they feel they are important to the life of the church? In my own situation we have developed a monthly 'Family Service', which is geared to the children. The service is deliberately short, children are allowed to go on walkabout, noise is not frowned upon and families take the prayers and the readings. Many families come to this service because they find a very relaxed and informal atmosphere. There are families who have joined the parish because of what they have found in this service. However, there are those families who only worship once a month. The title of 'Family Service' also concerns me because it may make single parent families feel uncomfortable and it may exclude those who are single or those who are childless.

I do believe we must find ways of engaging with our children; they are a wonderful gift to us. We must include them in our worship. Parents know the difficulty of children and the need for patience and tolerance when they make noise. We as a church must not make it difficult for families to come to worship. Within our own tradition of the Church of Ireland, the 'service of the word' allows for flexibility and creativity in these services that can be geared to children and families.

Within my own tradition another major issue that has caused great controversy is the struggle between the old prayer book and the new prayer book. There are congregations that only use one or the other. I worry that people exempt themselves from worship if a particular book is being used rather than the one they prefer. My predecessor in Ballyholme, Canon Jack Mercer, would not tell people which book would be used each Sunday because he told them they were not coming to worship a book but the almighty. We must find ways not to make the vehicle of worship more important than the act of worship. I declare my own interest in liturgical revision but I know there are those who prefer the older ways. These must be recognised and affirmed but it is unhelpful to argue over which makes worship more meaningful as this is something that is subjective. It will depend on our own experience, our own make-up and our own preferences as to which way we prefer to worship. We sometimes fail to find the value of a different way because we come to it with such closed minds. This is again one of the sins of our religious culture. We must not close our minds to experience old or new ways of worship.

The same principles apply to other arguments over worship. There is the argument over whether we prefer charismatic free worship to more traditional and formal worship. From those arguing for the free worship there is often the suggestion that free worship is much more spiritual than the formal. From those arguing for the formal worship there is the argument that the formal gives a sense of awe and reverence missing in the informal. These opinions are given to justify personal preference and may not be true. These issues can so easily be just our own opinion and preferences being justified. For everyone who comes to worship there will be different needs, different preferences and different aspects of worship that they find helpful. 'Worship is always contextualised, so no one style should be regarded as normative or more spiritual than another. What turns on some people is likely to put off others.' (*Church Next*, Coffey and Gibbs, page 155.)

To try to hold these together for many different people is probably an impossible task. The person who leads this community is shaped by their own preferences and by the group who shout the loudest. It is critical we find ways of engaging members of the congregation in formulating and discussing the ways we worship. We need to hear what people are saying. We need to understand the different needs of different people at different times in their lives. We must not exclude people because we allow a very limited diet of worship.

I have come to the conclusion that an *à la carte* menu is the best way to try to offer choice. At each service there should be different styles and different experiences of worship. In Ballyholme we have three different morning services offering different ways people can worship. The choice becomes one that people themselves make and is not one forced upon them because there is only a *table d'hote* menu. In the evening services we also try to offer variety ranging from Taizé services, choral evensong, compline and an informal service led by members of the congregation. I am sure there are those who would want more flexibility, as there are those who do not like so much variety.

These choices are possible partly because we have a very creative and talented organist. Ian Bell is willing and able to offer these different styles.

It is also important to get people to discuss these issues, as that will help people on this journey of choice. For those of us who are ordained, we need to find a more collaborative approach to these issues. We need to share leadership on the subject of worship. In our own diocese we have been asked to formulate a parish strategy for the next five years. Within our strategy, we have decided to form a worship group who will be representative of different views on worship. It will be important for people to hear what others say on the subject. This should help us evolve our worship over the next five years.

However, I want to leave the last comment on this to William Temple: 'Worship is the submission of all our nature to God. It is the quickening of conscience by his holiness; the nourishment of mind with his truth; the purifying of imagination by his beauty; the opening of the heart to his love; the surrender of will to his purpose – and all this gathered up in adoration, the most selfless emotion of which our nature is capable and therefore the chief remedy for that self-centredness which is our original sin and the source of all actual sin.' (*Readings in St John's Gospel*, William Temple, page 68.)

CHAPTER 9

Telling the Story

I only became acquainted with the novels of Anthony Trollope after I was ordained and I still find they make me smile. They give insights into the humanness of the church and particularly the frailty of the clergy. They also give some wonderful thoughts or views from the pew. In *Barchester Towers* the following comments are made on the subject of preaching and preachers:

There is, perhaps, no greater hardship at present inflicted on mankind in civilised and free countries, than the necessity of listening to sermons. No-one but a preaching clergyman has, in these realms, the power of compelling an audience to sit silent, and be tormented. No one but a preaching clergyman can revel in platitudes, truisms and untruisms, and yet receive, as his undisputed privilege, the same respectful demeanour as though words of impassioned eloquence, or persuasive logic fell from his lips. Let a professor of law or physic find his place in a lecture room, and there pour forth jejune words and empty phrases, and he will pour them forth to empty benches. Let a barrister attempt to talk without talking well, and he will talk but seldom. A judge's charge need be listened to perforce by none but the jury, prisoner and gaoler. A member of Parliament can be coughed down or counted out. Town councillors can be tabooed. But no one can rid himself of the preaching clergyman. He is the bore of the age ... the nightmare that disturbs our Sunday's rest, the incubus that overloads our religion and makes God's service distasteful. We are not forced into church! No: but we desire not to be forced to stay away. We desire, nay, we are resolute, to enjoy the comfort of public worship; but we desire also

that we may do so without an amount of tedium which ordinary human nature cannot endure with patience; that we
may be able to leave the house of God without that anxious
longing for escape, which is the common consequence of
common sermons. (*Barchester Towers*, pages 46-7.)

Perhaps this may produce a few echoes in the minds of
many. In fairness, there are preachers who do not enjoy the
struggle of preaching every Sunday and sometimes twice on a
Sunday. Part of the difficulty is that preparation time is limited
because of everything else that needs to be done.

One of the debates that are important to people on sermons is
the length of a sermon. There are those who think that a short
sermon, anything less than fifteen minutes, could not possibly
be doing much more than sharing a few thoughts. There are
those who think that once a sermon goes beyond fifteen minutes
it has completely lost the listeners. I believe that this argument is
not the important one. There are more important questions to be
asked. What is the sermon for or why do we preach? What is the
authority for what we say? Does preaching make any difference
to the hearers? These questions can be phrased in different
ways. My central concern is that those who preach have sometimes lost confidence in the very concept of preaching and/or
confidence in their ability to preach.

'Preaching is more than a little chat, a few sentences from the
chancel steps hastily thought up and indifferently delivered.'
(*New day for Preaching*, Donald Coggan, page 4.) The *Dictionary of
Christian Theology* states: 'Preaching consists in one thing only:
the exposition of the Word of God as contained in the scripture
in such a way as to bring home its saving and liberating truth to
the hearers, enabling them to understand that truth in relation to
the situation of their daily lives in the world which Christ came
to redeem and in which those who are in Christ are called to
serve.'

There are many issues raised by this definition. I want to
focus first on the need to make the scripture relevant to people's
daily lives. It is the relevance that is fundamental. How do we

take words that are from another culture and millennium and make them help somebody live out their life on Monday morning? How can people come out of church with thoughts to mull over and put into practice?

Westerhoff writes: 'We must begin to search for the metaphors, the images, and the strategies that will make the Christian life of faith meaningful for human beings in our era.'

Preaching is not about the preachers parading their learning. It is not about making logical abstract points about a certain passage of scripture. It is about helping the very life of scripture to impact upon people's lives. This is the work of the Holy Spirit. As Donald Coggan writes: 'When the preaching takes place, the main actor is not the preacher, nor the congregation but the Holy Spirit.'

However, we still need to focus on scripture. Our role is not to prove by various arguments or theories that Jonah was actually swallowed by a fish. Whether Jonah was swallowed by a fish or not is not the main reason for us learning from the truth of this book. Whether the book is a parable or an actual story is not the main thought behind this story, and will certainly not make Monday morning any easier. However, if I can learn that I will never find any peace or fulfilment until I discover and do the Lord's will, then I will have found something to bring with me. What the scriptures teach us about living the faith is what I must teach and preach. We need to engage with scripture to help people see how the faith can and does impinge upon all of life. 'As preachers sit at their desks, trying to think theologically, they hear with their minds the cries of the refugees bereft of home and hope, of women assaulted and raped, of children abused by their parents or dying for lack of food and medical aid. They see, with the eyes of their minds, the tragedy of the poor little rich men of the West, possessing all that money can buy and not knowing where to find peace. They read of the number of suicides, and note that the rate seems to be highest where scientific sophistication is at its peak. How, in God's name, are they to relate the truths of their theology to the realities which cry out to him from radio and television, from the press, and from the home of Mr and Mrs Jones down the road near the vicarage? Here the two worlds meet. Here is perplexity. Here also is the power of the gospel.' (*A New day for Preaching*, Donald Coggan, page 65.)

It is this grappling with scripture and the world in which we live that can bring depth and meaning to preaching. The relevance of preaching to peoples' lives is critical or else the faith will appear archaic and irrelevant. The truths of scripture will always be relevant but it is how we present them that can make the difference. This is a huge task and it must not be understated. The imagery and thought forms of the biblical writers are very different from our culture and way of thinking. It is easy to use religious jargon and to fail to grasp the original nuances and meanings. We can easily fail to understand the cultural implications of the events and stories. Yet we have to bridge that gap between the first century and the twenty-first century. For this to happen we need time to read, to pray and to prepare. Sermons may only take minutes to preach but they take hours to prepare. The scriptures must impact upon us before they can impact upon others through our preaching.

There may be those who are unhappy about my emphasis upon scripture. However, I have no other authority by which I can preach. At my ordination I certainly promised to preach using scripture as my authority. There is a struggle here with biblical criticism. There was a danger in my training that the scriptures were so taken apart with biblical criticism, which was somewhat out of date, that there was little confidence left in the scripture. I also believe some fundamentalist thinking has refused to engage with some of the difficulties of biblical studies. The creation story is one of the easiest examples. There are those who still want to argue that God made the world in seven days. How can this be aligned with scientific discoveries? I do believe that Genesis tells us God created the world but it does not tell us how it happened. It was written not as a scientific textbook but as a poetic description of God's dealings with his creation.

I believe very passionately that it is the scriptures that must be our authority for preaching. I also believe that the Holy Spirit takes my words and gives life to them to help others. However, I still have the hard work of studying, reading, praying and engaging with the world then and the world now in such a way that people can find God's word for them on a Monday morning and the rest of their week. Who would be a preacher?

It is imperative for preachers that we free our minds of our own personal agendas. There is a danger that we can use the scripture to say virtually anything we want it to. We must not become so fixated with certain issues or doctrines that we say what we want to say to people. 'In preparing to teach, we must free our minds of personal agendas and past experience, then permit our subject matter to engage us until it provides us with an insight into how it might engage others.' (*Spiritual life*, Westerhoff, page 26.)

There is also the danger of answering questions people are not asking. We need to find ways of hearing the questions that people are asking and the struggles they are having living their faith. Some of this comes through our pastoral work and experience. It may also be reading the daily newspaper or listening to radio or television news and current affairs. I found it invaluable to lead an Alpha course as it helped me to hear questions from people who were struggling with many questions. It also affected our subject matter for six months preaching.

As a helpful reflection I try to examine Jesus' preaching style. He would tell a story and leave the hearer to work out the meaning. The hearers were given respect and freedom to think for themselves. He rarely explained his stories. He often refused to answer a direct question but would reply with another question. He focused on the kingdom of God and how we are to find it, know it and live it out. The very clear focus allowed people space to respond, to question and to think for themselves. I worry that in our preaching we fail to leave space for questions or give space for people to think for themselves. Richard A. Bower of Trinity Church, Princeton, New Jersey, wrote: 'Like most matters of faith, preaching is meant to deepen questions more than produce answers. No preacher can work it all out for you. Responsibility and decision rest in your lap (or heart). So when we as preachers are doing our job, we are holding up the light of God's word with a minimum of our own light in ways that leave you the work to do, the response to make, the new questions to bring, the new hope to act upon.' (Quoted in Donald Coggan, page 32-3.)

Preachers need to respect their hearers. We must not harangue them or dump any more guilt upon them. My mum used to say: 'I don't go to church to hear how bad I am. I know that already. I go to see if I can be better.' There is also the danger that we talk to our hearers as if we are above this teaching. We are always preaching to ourselves. In this context I believe it is helpful when we can admit that we may finds things difficult. I know from comments I have received from people that they have been affirmed when I have admitted that I struggle with my own journey. As human beings, we often assume that we are the only one who finds things difficult, and it is liberating when we find that we are not alone.

This also raises the question of the relationship between the preacher and the congregation. In a booklet published by the British Council of Churches called *Views from the Pews*, the following statement was made: 'Theology has come to be regarded as a mystery which can be unravelled only by experts, and therefore the average members of the church are not expected to have any theological insights.' (Published 1986). The report also states: 'There is still a great deal of archaic (and therefore unintelligible) terminology used in churches … It was strongly recommended that such language be replaced by contemporary words and modern idiom.' This could easily become an argument over language. There are those who think that modern language is a very poor substitute for the King James Version. However, this is not a debate about language but about people finding their faith being nurtured by sermons they can understand and relate to. We do need to unpack the terms that are so often used in churches.

The community of faith or the local church needs to see that the sermon is something they participate in. We are all on a journey of faith and need to hear what God is saying to us all. 'The preacher who genuinely believes preaching is the activity of the whole congregation will not only develop the skills for a style of preaching which makes that possible but will also be patient while the listeners overcome years of quiet submission to someone else's conclusions.' (*Preaching,* F. B. Craddock.) The congregation have such an important role to play. Therefore they need to be given avenues to ask their questions and to comment on the preacher and style and content.

Let me make a few practical suggestions at this point. As part of our diocesan continuing ministerial education programme (this is some further training given to anyone in his or her first three years of ordained ministry), everyone is asked to complete a sermon assessment. This is a process of asking three or four parishioners to assess a couple of sermons that are preached by the curates. These are people who are hand picked and will be trusted to criticise but to do it constructively. It is suggested that the rectors have no part in this process. It appears to have been a very helpful exercise. It is interesting to hear if people have heard what you think you said. Are there any habits or mannerisms that are unhelpful? I have tried this exercise myself and found it very stimulating. It also affirms the truth that we are all involved in this gift of preaching. It may also be useful to ask a few people in the pew to answer a few pertinent questions. What are their expectations from a sermon? What are the critical issues facing them in everyday discipleship? How can preaching be made more relevant? The questions are not the important focus but rather the fact that clergy and people can discuss the subject together. I am always very conscious that one word of criticism bites very deeply into the spirit. Alternatively one word of affirmation can be so encouraging.

In terms of trying to discuss content and style, that is a more subjective issue. Yet the style of Jesus appears to give useful clues. He told stories that were based on everyday life. Stories that people could relate to and use as coat hangers for further reflection. When he told the parable of the sower there was probably a sower sowing seed in the background somewhere. When he told the story of the Good Samaritan people were shocked by the radical nature of what he was saying. When he told the story of the 'forgiving father' people understood the cultural nuances of the story, not least the role of the father as he 'ran' to meet his son.

I believe that we must tell stories that people can relate to – stories that come from the twenty-first century, and even better if they can be personal moments or stories. We can make the mistake of telling stories or using illustrations, and then spending so much time explaining them, that we have destroyed their usefulness. We must respect people's ability to do their own thinking with only some guidance.

There is one thing I want to try when I go back to preaching, after this sabbatical. I want occasionally to preach a sermon and allow people to interrupt me with questions or comments. I am sure many people come to worship and go away frustrated because they disagreed or were completely lost by what was said, perhaps bored might be more honest. I want to engage with the community of faith in order that we can all learn together. It might sound intimidating for the preacher, but if they trust me every week to preach, I need to trust them to question.

John Stott makes the following comment on preaching: 'Whatever is dull, drab, dowdy, slow or monotonous cannot compete in the television age. Television challenges preachers to make our presentation of the truth attractive through variety, colour, illustration, humour and fast flowing movement. And in addition, although nothing can supplant preaching, it definitely needs to be supplemented.' (*I Believe in Preaching*, J. Stott, page 76.) The content of a sermon may be important and helpful but if the delivery is drab it will not be heard as it should. The delivery could be excellent but the content weak. Content and delivery are both critical. We need to be sure that what we are saying is relevant but we need also to be sure that the delivery and style are such that people will hear it.

In my experience another helpful tool is the use of silence or the pause. Before I preach, I always stand quietly after the opening prayer. I want to engage the hearers. I want them to believe that what is to follow is important. Throughout the sermon the use of silence or a pause is useful. It can let people catch up, gather their thoughts and help the preacher realise if they are still listening. 'While we preach we will receive countless signals in body language and in other ways of how the faithful are responding to what we are saying. This means that we should never be so bound to a manuscript that we lose our freedom to respond to the messages we are receiving from the faces turned towards us.' (*Elements of Homiletic*, O. C. Edwards Jr., page 97.) As we minister in a particular place these messages become easier to read and we ignore them at our peril. If people are not listening we need to know why they are not. There may be good reasons for the reaction especially if the message is an uncomfortable one. However, it may be that they have not understood our logic.

Preaching is a massive responsibility and a wonderful privilege. For me it highlights the frustration and fulfilment of ordained ministry. The frustration may not just be for those who are ordained. As Trollope rightly comments, no other profession is given the privilege of being heard without comment or question. The right to be heard has to be earned and must not be assumed. I do recommend the use of sermon assessment by those who preach with those who can give constructive criticism in the context of affirmation.

CHAPTER 10

Shepherd or Sheep Dog?

From a very young age I was given a love of football. For some people who know me that might read as an understatement. I have an amazing passion for the game. I love talking about it, trying to play it and watching it. As a child this would include kicking tin cans to improve my aim, kicking a ball against a wall and playing football before, during and after school. Holes in the knees of my school trousers, scuffed shoes and various cuts and bruises were all part of playing the beautiful game. This information is important because it will make more sense of the story that follows.

I was playing in a cup final for the parish under-13 team. Someone who gave his life helping us play the game he loved managed our church football team. Jimmy Weir has since been heavily involved in making the annual Milk Cup in Northern Ireland such a great success. He was our coach and was every bit as passionate about the game as most of us were. This junior cup final was a very big moment for me. Every year I watched the FA Cup Final from Wembley and dreamed about one day playing in it. It was a glorious summer evening and I was playing in defence, left full back to be exact. There were those who might have said I should have been left back in the changing rooms because of what happened.

My boots were polished and our kit was spotless. Photographs were taken and we actually had a crowd of spectators, mostly families. It was a very tight game and everybody was cautious and nervous. I can still see the ball going over my head towards my goal as I turned to chase it, closely followed by an opponent. I got to the ball first and kicked it back to our goalkeeper. It was a wonderful strike right over the goalie's head into the top right hand corner of the net. It was a brilliant own goal. I felt sick and my team-mates were not very supportive. I wanted the ground to swallow me up. I have never felt so humiliated. At that moment in my football career the words of Bill Shankly were very apt: 'Football is not a matter of life and death. It is more important than that.'

Half time came and we were still losing by that great own goal. You can imagine the banter, the comments and the abuse I received from the rest of the team. Actually I thought I played quite well apart from that mistake, although it was a major *faux pas*. Then having listened to the team for a short while the coach came to my rescue. I cannot remember his exact words but I can remember the essence of what he said. The midfield had given the ball away. The defence were not marking their forwards tightly enough. The strikers had missed two or three chances. The goalkeeper was too far out of his goal. We had all made mistakes and it was the team that was to blame for us losing, not one person who had made a mistake. He told me, 'Next time play safe. Just kick it out of play.' The team was silenced and they all looked a little sheepish. His final thought was a simple one, that if we lost, it would be because the team had lost, not just one person.

I do like happy endings and we scored two goals and won the game. I would love to say I scored the winning goal but I didn't.

The loneliness disappeared and we as a team had won and I had played my part. That victory was special. The prize was my first medal and I had learned an important lesson. Football is a team game and all the players have to play their part.

Yet I do remember the loneliness of feeling so responsible during the first half of the game. I had to take responsibility that was not mine but belonged to the whole team.

When I was ordained one of the great frustrations was feeling that same sense of responsibility for the church that was not mine but should be shared. I suddenly felt huge expectations being placed upon me and there was nowhere to hide. This was a very lonely experience. I was facing the prospect of being the one person who could minister, make decisions and yet who was accountable to so many people who did not share that responsibility.

I discovered there were those who were content to allow the clergy to take the lead, as long as it was in the direction they wanted to go. There were also those who wanted to control what you did by offering what might be called 'friendly advice'. Then there were those who did not want any responsibility as long as most people were satisfied. Within any parish or congregation there is such a wide variety of ideas and needs.

Over the years that I have been in the ordained ministry, I have increasingly believed in the need to develop and build a collaborative ministry in a parish. I did not want to continue with the loneliness and isolation of the 'one man band'. I do believe collaborative ministry is also a more biblical model of ministry. Much of the stress and isolation that come from ordained ministry come from the isolation and loneliness of being the one person through which all things must happen. It may not always be possible to get people to share the responsibility in parish life. It is certainly more risky to encourage people to share in the responsibility of making decisions, especially as they might disagree with you. However, I do believe it is how parish ministry must evolve for the spiritual and physical health of all involved in ministry, lay and ordained. Unfortunately there are no obvious structures for this to happen but new ways need to be found.

Over a period of decades, the work and witness of Jean Vanier has come to be recognised as an expression of the incarnate gospel. He has sought with others to live out the gospel with people who are mentally handicapped. I find his comments about leadership and community incisive and illuminating. In his book *Community and Growth* he writes: 'People with responsibility must always share their work, even if others do it less well than they do or in a different way. It is always easier to do things ourselves than to teach others to do them. People with responsibility who fall into the trap of wanting to do everything themselves are in danger of becoming isolated.' (*Community and Growth*, Jean Vanier, page 158.) This is one of the greatest tensions I have experienced in ordained ministry. It is often easier to do things yourself. It demands no trust or no vulnerability to do everything yourself but I believe I become the poorer for always doing things for others, rather than helping others share in ministry with me. As I learn to share the ministry I believe I find more fulfilment as others nurture my vocation.

In my training I was never taught on the subject of shared leadership. The impression was given that we had to be very careful whom we trusted and that ministry will always be lonely. Leadership will still have moments of being alone but the church must not be so dependent on one person. Especially from where I view this subject, that one person feels very inadequate.

John Goldingay in his Grove Booklet states the cause for shared leadership very starkly: 'This is not to say that the creative contribution of a gifted leader will not be of a key importance to the growth of a church; nor that a theologically equipped leader and teacher will not play a big part in the maturing of the church; nor that in our society a church may not function much more efficiently if it has a full time stipendiary executive officer; nor even (for the sake of argument) that the presidency at the Eucharist may not be located at least normally in one particular person. It is rather to say that we should not look for all these functions to be fulfilled by the same person, but rather that its elders should exercise genuine corporate leadership of the local church. There is no place for the traditional concept of the clergyman.' (*Authority and Ministry*, Grove Booklet 24, John Goldingay.)

As I reflect on twenty years of ordination, I am very aware that it is this model of ministry that I inherited and that I really struggled with. I do not want to function as the one who tries to do the ministry; it is something I actually cannot do. Yet there is the danger that this is what some people expect from those who are ordained. As there are no obvious alternative models the frustration grows in this struggle. It has at times made me question the very vocation that brought me here in the first place.

I have always believed that my role is that expressed in Ephesians 4 verses 11 and 12: 'It was he who gave some to be apostles, some to be prophets, some to be evangelists, and some to be pastors and teachers, to prepare God's people for works of service, so that the body of Christ may be built up.'(NIV) *The Message*, written by Eugene Peterson, has a different emphasis: 'He handed out gifts of apostle, prophet, evangelist and pastor-teacher to train Christians in skilled servant work, working within Christ's body the church, until we're all moving rhythmically and easily with each other.' As someone who is called to leadership within the church I believe one of my main goals must be to equip others for the work of ministry. Graham Cray, in an address I heard him give when he was vicar of St Michael-Le-Belfry in York, said the following: 'Leadership is a specific role of ministry within the body of Christ, not a specific status. It is not a matter of controlling the people of God, but of equipping them … All ministry has the same status, but leadership has the special role of serving the people of God so that they may all minister and coordinate their individual ministries to fulfil a common vision.'

Inevitably this thinking will lead to various tensions in the lives of those who are ordained. In the New Testament leadership appears to have been recognised in the local community and then publicly given official authority. In the life of those who are ordained, we arrive in a local community and have to discern what the important issues are in the local situation. Often as I have visited I have been told, 'I belong to your church, rector'. The parish is never mine and the local people have to take responsibility with me for what happens in it. For this shared leadership to take place we have to build trust between clergy and people. It is trust that will enable new models to be implemented and changes to be made. This is a slow and tedious process.

When I first became a rector I received a letter that I have found so helpful ever since. It came from someone who is now a bishop in the Church of Ireland. Bishop Ken Clarke, affectionately known as 'Fanta', wrote the following: 'Remember more than anything else, your people must know that you love them and that you are on their side.' This expresses something that is at the heart of parochial life and ministry. The people in any parish must believe that their clergy are trying to do what is best for parish and people. Clergy must not always be scolding, chastising or bullying people into accepting their agenda. Trust is what allows change to take place and because of the nature of our structures that trust is best brought about by a pastoral care offered when people are in grief and pain. If we as clergy are there for people when they are in need, I believe we can then earn the right to be listened to and trusted.

When changes are being made communication is critical, communication that allows people space and time to think through what is happening. 'Real communication happens when people feel safe ... Find ways to convince your people that you mean them no harm ... Leadership is not something you do to people. It's something you do with people.' (*The heart of a Leader*, Ken Blanchard, page 71.) When trust is developed and people are given the space to express their views, change can be handled with care, although not without some difficulties. It is important as a leader to receive feedback and to know how others view your leadership and ministry.

It is not easy to hear criticism, yet it is important to reflect upon how we deal with negative voices and comments. I have often made the mistake of taking the comments personally. This in turn leads to self-doubt and insecurity. I certainly look back on ministry and wonder what has been the affect on me of having been ordained. Certainly I have found myself emotionally drained. My spirituality and inner resources have been stretched to the limit. Doubts and questions on matters of faith have loomed large and I have been uncertain how to face them. The criticism of others has left me feeling empty and angry. I certainly need to find ways of hearing negative comments and learning from them. There is the need for an environment where I can hear comments and thoughts from others in the context of shared leadership. The crux of this issue is summed up in the writing of Ken Blanchard: 'I go out into the world every day with the attitude that my "okayness" is not up for grabs. I firmly believe that "God did not make junk". This doesn't mean I don't have areas of my life that need improvement – just that at my basic core, I'm okay.' There are many in the ordained ministry who have had their 'okayness' questioned by people or by how the establishment has treated them. It is fundamental to survival and fulfilment in ministry that we believe and know that nobody can take away what God has given to us. He has called us and declared us worthy even though we feel we are not. We must not lose sight of where our real value and worth comes from.

As I have sought to share leadership in parochial ministry, there are key principles that appear to have emerged. These have emerged as I look back rather than ones that were thought through carefully and planned. Part of my difficulty in leadership has always been that I have a dream of an inclusive, reconciling, worshipping and caring community that impacts upon the local community but I have no idea how to get there. It has meant that, for me, leadership has been haphazard and trying to learn on the job.

Hans Küng, in his book *Why Priests?*, makes the following terse comment about ordination: 'A bishop can never replace the Spirit of Christ by merely laying on his hands. If the Spirit is absent, he can never simply commission for the work of leadership those who happen to suit him and who do what he wants. When all human calls have been heard, if the call of God is missing, despite all ordination ceremonies the shepherd will prove to be a hireling.' I have to remind myself frequently of the fact that God called me to do this. I keep a photograph of the chapel in St Bartholomew's Hospital in London in my study, as a reminder of that moment many years ago when I was aware of his peace moving me towards my ordination. I am rector in a parish, not because I want to be or because a board of nomination chose me, but because many years ago I responded to his call. I have also found it useful on the anniversary of my ordination to pray my vows again. It has also been helpful on the anniversary of my institution to pray my promises again. I am serving in this ministry because God has called me, and as he has called me, he will enable me to do what I am called to do. It is rather like a pact I have with God. Since I believe that he has a wonderful sense of humour, it helps me to think this way. He has got me into this mess, so it is his problem to see I get through it as best I can with his help. So far I have found that he has not let me down.

In each parish and church community there is the need to discover a vision of what is meant to be happening in the life of the faith community. This comes from our belief that we are called by God to live out the faith in our own situation. We are to be the salt and the light wherever we are called to serve him and others. Leadership then involves helping the local church to discover the vision that God might have for us. In each situation this will be affected by circumstances and by the leaders who are in place. 'A clear vision is really just a picture of how things would be if everything were running as planned ... Dreams lift us up. If we really believe them, we start acting as if they are already true.'(*The heart of a Leader,* Ken Blanchard, page 83.) It is critical to enable as many people as possible to share in this vision. The informal conversations, visits, cups of coffee, lunches and personal contacts are how the vision can be shared. The vision can be shaped and moulded and as many as possible then can take ownership of it as it evolves.

The sharing of people in this vision is an important part of leadership. 'Good leaders glean information and welcome opinions from a variety of sources. To understand their organisation better they talk to a wide cross-section of people – a diagonal slice of it.' The Old Testament prophets were leaders who understood their local community and issues. 'The prophets were astute observers of what was happening on the national and international scene, seeing behind external religious observance to moral and spiritual realities, discerning God's hand in the rise and fall of the nations.' (Both quotes from *Transforming Leadership*, Richard Higginson, page 88.) Knowing parish and people is critical in the leadership needed in a faith community that is the parish or congregation. Certainly within our present structures in the Church of Ireland the main source of this is the hard slog of pastoral care. Within my present parish in Ballyholme it has also been vital to involve a cross-section of views as we attempt to move forward.

As part of our diocesan strategy for the first five years of the new millennium our bishop has asked every parish in the diocese to formulate a five-year strategy for their own situation. The suggested method for doing this was to form a strategy group in each parish. In our own parish we had a support group who had formulated a five-year strategy that had brought us towards the year 2000. This had consisted of the four parochial nominators who had helped bring me to Ballyholme. This group of four had been supplemented with the addition of two outgoing rector's churchwardens. Churchwardens are people who are meant to hold office in the parish for a year and are to help with the ordering of worship every Sunday. This group had helped formulate a strategy entitled 'Towards 2000', which had largely been implemented. A new group with an overlap of one person formulated our new strategy as requested by the bishop. When the new strategy was being discussed the old support group met with the new group to discuss the new ideas and see how they fitted into the journey that our parish was taking. The strategy was also discussed in depth by the select vestry and sent to every home in the parish for comment before being finalised. The following is the final format of our strategy for the next five years. More important than the strategy is the process that enabled it to come into being.

PARISH STRATEGY DOCUMENT

Aim 1: To foster fellowship with God and one another.

Goals:

From January 2000 when there is a fifth Sunday we will unite the 10.00 and 11.30 am services to enable people to worship together. This service would be at 11.00 am and attempt to bring together different strands and styles of worship. This will be followed by coffee or a bread and cheese lunch and money will be donated to charity.

To form a development group to reflect upon all our worship and the needs of all people.

To continue to develop and expand our house groups.

To look at ways of developing people's awareness of how important holy communion is in our tradition.

Specific goals for 2000
To have three meetings of the development group and produce a report for the strategy group.
To develop a new house group and a programme for house group leaders training.

Aim 2: To encourage people to grow in their faith and to develop their talents within the life and faith of the church and to identify other needs of the parish, e.g. children.

Goals:

To mobilise the resources we have for the needs of the parish.

To involve many more people in the work of the parish.

To further develop a network of care for our senior parishioners.

To plan and develop a pastoral network for all our parishioners.

Specific goals for 2000
Assessment of how a pastoral network can be formed, resourced and managed. Report by November 2000.

Assessment of elderly provision and needs. To also develop structure for helping. Report by November 2000.

Aim 3: To ensure we as a parish develop our involvement in local, national and world needs.

Goals:

Local: To affirm and expand the existing local inter-church contacts.

To investigate the possibility of an inter-church project for the community.

National: To examine the possibility of becoming involved in the Habitat Community Housing project.

To examine how we might engage in the real difficulty of reconciliation – perhaps linking with a Roman Catholic parish elsewhere in the province.

World: To continue our link with and support for Bishop Balya College, Uganda.

To develop further contacts with the worldwide church.

To look at and encourage the possibility of trips in both directions.

Specific goals for 2000

Arrange a Saturday trip in the year 2000 – to Habitat for Humanity in Belfast.

The hope is that more and more people will begin to share in the ministry of the parish. There are many people who worship on Sundays. However, they appear to find it difficult, because of our structures or of their reticence, to be involved in any more. In this process of finding vision and direction, consultation has been important. The strategy group took nearly a year to formulate their ideas and everyone in the parish was given an opportunity to comment on the strategy. 'Consultation is nearly always a must in order to show respect, keep morale and confidence high, and glean good ideas about how change can be carried out smoothly and effectively.' (*Transforming Leadership*, Higginson, pages 92-93.)

On this journey of consultation I found that affirmation was key. Everyone involved in this process must be affirmed. Too often in church life people can be scolded or made to feel guilty because they are not doing what is expected of them. I believe that people who come to church today come because they choose to be there, and they need to be appreciated. We as clergy need to be affirmed. It is my experience that as I offer affirmation I am more likely to receive it. We need to create a culture of affirmation. We need to: 'encourage one another and build one another up.' (1 Thess 5:11) To anyone who has the care of those who are ordained, please affirm and encourage them; they then may be able to hear any constructive criticism you may have. Too often clergy only hear the negative messages, as they are the most vocal and strident. Negative messages stay in the mind much longer than positive messages. If people could realise the damage that can be done to the spirit of those who are there to serve them, they might be more careful in what they say and how they say it. To those who are ordained, do not harangue or bully your people, love and encourage them into life. If things get very desperate the biblical injunction may be appropriate: 'shake the dust off your feet.' (Matthew 10:14.)

In being ordained there is also the danger that we can compare ourselves with others who are ordained. We can feel inadequate because we think we are not as good a leader as someone else. We may think we are not as successful as someone else although how we measure success is a difficult issue. It is important that we recognise that there are different styles of leadership and these are often a matter of personality and temperament. 'Different people exercise authority in different ways, according to their own temperaments. Some people are leaders and have a creativity, which gives them vision of the future: they lead from the front. Others are more shy and humble: they walk among others and make excellent coordinators. The essential for all with authority is that they are servants before they are bosses. People who assume responsibility to prove something, because they tend to be dominating and controlling, because they need to see themselves at the top or because they are looking for privileges and prestige, will always exercise their responsibility badly. They must first want to be servants.' (*Community and Growth*, Jean Vanier, page 152.) The greatest gift we bring to ministry is the gift of ourselves. We need to allow ourselves the freedom to lead in the way that is right for us.

In the New Testament there are three main words used for those who are in leadership or responsibility: servant, shepherd and steward. The steward is someone who is entrusted with something that belongs to his master. Those in leadership are stewards of what must always be seen as belonging to God. The church is not ours but his. The people that I am responsible for are his and not mine. As stewards we are called to be faithful.

The analogy of the shepherd brings a sense of intimacy to bear on leadership and ministry. We are there to care, to love, to feed, to help all and to be there for those not of the fold. In the difficult and painful moments we must be there to care for the sheep.

Servants are to model leadership and ministry by being the servant of all. The word used in the New Testament for servant is translated 'slave'. We must be careful not to use our position to further our own needs and agenda. We are to help others find their potential in him. Leadership in the Christian Church must follow the example of the one who modelled leadership for us in the most profound way. It led him to a piece of wood in the form of a cross.

In conclusion, it is important to focus on what is at the heart of what it is to be in leadership in the church. Leslie Newbigin writes: 'Ministerial leadership is, first and finally, discipleship.' (*The Gospel in a Pluralist Society*, Newbigin, page 241.) As I have reflected upon my ministry I am in no doubt that the greatest danger has been that I can lose sight of what matters most, my relationship with Jesus. He is the one who has called me, the one who equips me and enables me. He is the one who can help me be a servant, shepherd and steward. He is the one who helps me find fulfilment amid the many frustrations of working within a structure of ministry that often makes the vision of shared leadership and collaboration difficult to implement.

However, I end this chapter with a beautiful picture of the church as a community with everyone having a part to play. Jean Vanier paints the picture in words: 'A community is like an orchestra: each instrument is beautiful when it plays alone, but when they all play together, each given its own weight in turn, the result is even more beautiful. A community is like a garden full of flowers, shrubs and trees. Each helps give life to the other. Together, they bear witness to the beauty of God, creator and gardener – extraordinary.'

CHAPTER 11

Searching for Change

From my early years in ministry I have always struggled with the model of church I was forced to work with. My conviction and belief has always been that all of God's people have gifts to help them play their part within the life of the church. In the words of Cardinal Suenens: 'The church is the people of God together: all the baptised living in co-responsibility.' (*The future of the Christian Church*, Cardinal Suenens, page 84.) I increasingly have come to understand the words of Michael Harper when he wrote 'that any notion of the one-man ministry is doomed to failure.' (*Let my People Grow*, Michael Harper, page 150.) Those who have to sit in the pew and are often unable to offer their ministry share this frustration. 'Why is it that the church today will not trust its members? Why does the church so often decline to recognise and accept the activity of the Spirit among unregulated groups of Christians? Why is it all initiative in the church is presumed to derive from the clergy?' (*The People's Church*, George Gayder, page 55.)

Over the last few decades the shortage of clergy has sharpened this issue more clearly. 'The ... church will have to take for granted reduced numbers of stipendiary clergy and will not be able financially to maintain the old infrastructures.' (*Practising Community*, R. Greenwood, page 60.) Throughout history, in each and every generation, the church has had to find ways of making sense of the culture of the day and at the same time present the message of God's revelation in Jesus. In essence, the church has had to find ways of being the church. Sometimes this has meant rediscovering facets of the message that had been forgotten. It has also meant discovering new elements of what it is to be the church. I find it encouraging as I seek to discover new ways of being church to remember that it is not my church. 'The church itself is thus not a sacred trust given to one generation to be handed on to the next, or a human institution to be carefully guarded or even carefully reformed for human purposes. The church today, as much as at the church at Pentecost, is constituted by and utterly dependent upon the Holy Spirit.' (*Shaping our Future,* J. S. Freeman, page 29.) We need to seek the help of the Holy Spirit in all we try to do and try to discover where he might be leading.

It is also important to state that in general terms the church in Ireland, as we know it, is in decline. There are fewer people attending worship and fewer people are claiming to have a Christian faith. Churches have closed, parishes have been grouped together and overall numbers are in decline. There may be exceptions to this trend but generally we are not a growing church. In fact the church as I experience it is being marginalised and the perception of those outside the church is that it is irrelevant and therefore the same applies to the message it proclaims. It is critical that the church at large is able to admit that there are serious problems to be addressed. It is also important that, when issues are addressed, they are handled carefully. One sure way to make life difficult is for clergy to arrive in parishes and immediately make wholesale changes. If consultation and listening does not take place there will probably be a vehement reaction against anything new. We are dealing with an institution which by its very nature is conservative. We are living in a society that is finding change in so many areas of life threatening and the church is often viewed as a safe place where everything stays the same.

Whatever changes are made must come about from a process of reflection and discernment. Every situation is different, with context and needs forming a basis from which a vision can be clarified. Also, different people will have different thoughts on what the role of the church should be. The interpretation of scripture will also play a part in this process. As many people as possible have to engage with this process of discovering a vision and purpose. There will be some who are content with the status quo. There will be those who want to be very radical and are unrealistic in their expectations. Somehow these different views must find ways of disagreeing to find a common purpose. Critical to this must be the clear understanding that the ordained person must not be the only person concerned about these issues. There must be a shared leadership where the ordained person will probably be the leader but all must know the vision and the strategy for change. There must also be the recognition by those in leadership that we are not always certain what to do but that we are trying to move forward together.

It has proved to be of great benefit since, but at the time I did not talk about it at home. I was in sixth form in school and with others had just discovered the delights of free periods. This was meant to be time to study, to use the library or even to do homework. These were obviously very good guidelines but at sixteen seemed a little bit serious. There were a few of us who enjoyed the delight of playing cards. This was even more fun when you played for matchsticks. I was too terrified to play for money after what happened to my dad. However there were occasions when money passed hands between some of the card sharks. We were discovered playing cards in one of the empty classrooms of our new purpose built sixth form centre, during one of our free periods. We then discovered the joy of creative punishment. We were instructed that the reward for our misdemeanour was to stay behind after school one afternoon a week to learn the delights of playing bridge. I have loved the game ever since. This was to be seen by us as a useful exercise. Bridge became a new hobby and interest.

In the context of the crime, our age, our educational development and our need for re-direction, this was a wonderful lesson in management. Context is critical as we seek to bring about any changes. The society in which we live and work is changing rapidly and we need to discern what is our role as the church within that. We also need to recognise that many within our

culture have grown weary with religious clichés. Many have
had an overdose of what can best be described as negative religion. I meet many people who have been brought up with a very
religious childhood and they have been glad to break free from
the confines and negativity of what they saw as the faith. Within
the church there is also the context of a natural conservatism.
New ideas are frowned upon and they may even be viewed as
suspect or liberal. Various church groups have been able to try
new things and to be more radical in their approaches. These
groups have often started with a committed group of people
who decide to be church in their situation, or they have started
with an empty building facing closure. They have not had to
deal with the inbuilt reaction to progress.

I want to sound a note of caution at this point. There is always
a danger that we can look at other models of what churches are
doing in very different contexts and try to copy what they are
doing in our own situation. I believe that every situation is different and we cannot copy others but we can learn lessons and
share ideas. If we copy from other situations, the cultural differences and the fact that change has not been properly processed
can lead to change that does not have deep roots and it will be
resisted more strongly than it might have been. We must find
ways of doing what we believe needs to be done in our own situation and, in doing so, to use the gifts and wisdom that we have
been given. To simply copy others seeks to shortcut the necessary process of making change more possible, applicable, permanent and relevant. We need to help as many as possible to
take ownership of moving into the future together.

In any journey of change it is helpful to face the reality of the
task. 'For the only place to start is where we are. Otherwise the
vision is never brought down to earth and consequently remains
in fantasy land.' (*Church Next*, Coffey and Gibbs, page 39.)

However, as well as facing the reality it is imperative to have
a vision for the future, which is different from the present. My
own vision has been shaped by years of working with the reality.
I do worry sometimes that it has been damaged by the enormity

of what needs to be done. My vision has still at its heart a church that is learning to share leadership, involve as many as possible in ministry and help as many as possible grow in personal and corporate faith and action. As I try to distil my own thoughts after years of practice there are some key areas in church life that need to be changed. There are also some aspects of church life that will make that very experimentation and alteration more difficult. I want to examine the latter first.

The church is an institution that at its core is conservative. 'Most churches are conservative by nature, and this has both positive and negative aspects. On the one hand, the long history of the church has built a store of experiences that cautions the present generation against simply noting every cultural wave that comes along for fear of being overwhelmed by it. On the other hand, the church is also called to relate the gospel to each cultural context in which it seeks to bear witness.' (*Church Next*, Coffey and Gibbs, page 36.) This conservative nature of the church has meant the church has rarely been proactive amidst the changes in society. The church is often simply reacting to them. This makes the church appear as reactionary and lacking in creative energy and drive. Those who are seeking to bring about change need immense patience and wisdom. Support structures and resources need to be offered to those who want to think creatively about the future ministry and life of the church but who seek to do so inside the discipline of the established churches.

Any process of transformation is actually very difficult for clergy to implement. 'For many, ministry roles have changed so dramatically that they are simply trying to hold on and survive.' (*The Missionary Congregation: Leadership and Liminality*, Alan J. Roxburgh, page 16.) It is also one of the weaknesses of training that clergy are not taught how to share leadership and involve the whole church where possible. The loneliness of the ordained ministry, when someone is vulnerable in seeking to be different and share, is difficult. Clergy are not trained to think creatively and strategically. Much of ordination training is about academic

learning in a limited theological field of study. There are real difficulties in applying any academic learning to the situation of
ministry that needs strategic thinking and planning. It has often
been said that clergy have been trained for maintenance rather
than mission. The difficulty with this is that we are maintaining
decline and not managing growth. Clergy have also been left
with an ever-increasing pastoral workload and expectations that
leave little or no time for the implementation of any innovative
ideas.

We need to discover ways of reflecting on what our role is, as
ordained and lay, within the ministry of the church. Part of this
reflection will be the recognition in more than just words that all
of God's people have a ministry. This will mean people in the
pew being given confidence and space to exercise their God
given ministry. It will also mean clergy being given the confidence and support to share leadership. 'We need to reclaim the
word vocation for the whole people of God ... to argue that the
vocation of the laity is crucial to the mission and ministry of the
church. Their calling is not secondary or subsidiary to that of the
clergy, it is just as important and equally valid.' (*Management
and Ministry,* ed. John Nelson, page 68.) There are dangers inherent within this as well. We must be careful not to make very
busy people even busier. The church can sometimes ask too
much of some people because they show ability or enthusiasm.
There is also the danger of creating a dichotomy between ministry in the church context and outside the church. All our lives,
whether ordained or lay, are our ministry.

In 1985 the General Synod Board of Education of the Church
of England published a report entitled *All are Called – Towards a
Theology of the Laity.* In this report there is a note of caution on
this subject. 'It has to be admitted that very many of our lay people would frankly "rather not be called". When they are told
they are "ministers" and a "royal priesthood", they do not wish
to be committed to such responsibilities.' There are many people
who want to find space and peace within the life of the church.
There are many who feel inadequate and unable to offer any-

thing of value. We must engage with the reality and part of this is a process of re-education for clergy and lay together.

Seeking to share leadership is not always easy. There are clergy who probably feel, 'It is always easier to do the job yourself than to delegate and have to pick up the pieces when the job has not been properly done. Sharing in leadership can also put excessive pressure on already deeply committed lay-people, on their families, and on their life at work.'(*All are Called*, page 54.) It is critical to define roles and expectations for all concerned in shared leadership. It also follows that affirmation and appreciation must be given to all involved. Taking people for granted is one of the greatest sins of the church.

As in all institutions, there will be those who want to suggest that there is no need for change. In fact there will be those who will argue that all we have to do is to return to the past and the glory days when everything was great. I call this selective re-membering. The church that charged people for their own particular pew, the church that lambasted any young girl who got pregnant outside wedlock, the church that had little compassion for divorcees and the church that survived a great deal on guilt cannot be the perfect church of yesteryear. My experience with people tells me that there are many people who were so sickened by compulsory religion as a child that they couldn't face going back. We as a church community have to find ways of engaging with the many people who no longer see the church as having anything to offer them in their search for meaning and purpose. We must be aware of the world outside the church and we must not be dependent on the clergy to help these people rediscover faith and life within the church. We must be open to innovation and be more flexible in our thinking and approach to people, and not become exclusive and even more irrelevant.

Having attempted to discuss some of the issues that make change more difficult, it would be useful to shift the spotlight to those areas where change is possible and where it would be constructive. I am not suggesting any kind of blueprint but rather sharing my experience of parish life as I have found it.

Within our culture today there has been an ever-increasing emphasis on the individual. 'In much of our society, with its emphasis on individuals standing on their own feet, the man would have been expected to sort out his own problems. In the Bible, as in rural countries today, orphans and old people would not be a charge on the community at large, because the extended family came to the rescue.' (*Built as a City*, D. Shepherd, page 333.) The community that I grew up in was a place where neighbour knew neighbour, where grandparents lived close by and where people didn't travel that far from home. Now I live in a society where communities have been decimated and polarised. The church has to challenge this by being community. 'God as love is experienced not in large organisations and institutions but in communities in which people can embrace each other.' (*The Open Church*, Moltmann, page 125.) Alan Ecclestone, writing in the *Church Times* in 1992, says something similar in his usual forthright manner: 'The church's real purpose should be a network of communities learning to love one another, leavening the whole populace and so transforming this devilish society we live in into something nearer the kingdom of God.' Leslie Newbigin, in his search for the presentation of the gospel in a pluralist society, argues that this community, that is the expression of church, is not just for its own members but also for the place in which it is called to serve. 'It will be a community that does not live for itself but is deeply involved in the concerns of its neighbourhood.'(*The Gospel in a Pluralist Society*, Newbigin, page 229.)

My experience convinces me of the need for congregations to grasp this concept of community. We belong to each other, we need each other and we need everyone to play their part. As we are more aware of community we can develop new forms of ministry. This will help us meet the needs of the church community and the wider community in which we are called to live and work. I have been very aware of the frustration I have felt that I have not had time to develop new ideas because the constant demands of a pastoral workload leave no time for anything other than reacting to need and pain.

In our parish setting at present our new strategy group have agreed that we need some kind of pastoral network to help us offer care to people in more manageable units. With one thousand family units in our parish, the idea is to divide the parish into one hundred and fifty units of eight or nine homes in each unit. This would be to develop a process of reactive care. It would mean having someone responsible for each unit that would help offer care to each household, especially in the crisis moments. The offers of help would range from providing a lift to hospital, doing some shopping, helping with childminding or helping collect someone's pension. In our present culture I believe parish communities must be more willing to bear one another's burdens and not expect a few to do it. I can empathise with the words of Eddie Gibbs and Ian Coffey: 'Especially burdensome for old-line churches are the large external constituencies consisting of inactive members who suddenly become "active" when they face a family crisis, when they are in need of a service from the church ... In an age when the family structure is under so much pressure, pastoral loads have increased. There are many dysfunctional families, young families without the support of the extended family, single parents and an ageing population ... In order to respond to so many pastoral demands, leaders must establish relational networks to provide the support everyone needs.' (*Church Next*, Coffey and Gibbs, page 73.)

The difficulty in a change like this is that even it is dependent upon one person making it happen. I look forward to trying to implement this, with the frustration and fulfilment that it will bring.

Within larger parishes there is also a struggle for people to find a place other than just being pew fillers on a Sunday. For some people in this situation small house groups have become a very positive way in which to become part of parish life in a more informal way. There are some who may find the very thought of house groups terrifying because they assume they are hotbeds of serious religion where everyone is very intense and the people spend all evening praying. My experience of house groups is that they can be a very helpful way of building community. They can help develop relationships between people on a journey of faith. People have different experiences of faith and the mutual sharing can be very encouraging. They can also be places where people find space to ask questions and express doubts. 'Small groups can be introduced without by-passing or undercutting the church ... The small group is best seen as an essential component of the church's structure and ministry, not as a replacement for the church.' (*The Problems of Wineskins: Church Structures in a Technological Age*, H. Synder, page 142.)

The church also needs to find ways of engaging with a society that has had a fill of religiosity and angry preachers who appear to have a very negative message. Some evangelism in our religious culture has also been seen as aggressive and harsh. Unfortunately this has meant that many in the church, including myself, have been very nervous in doing it at all. I have found the words of Eugene Peterson, in *The Message*, very helpful as a focus for my questioning on this subject: 'Even though I am free of the demands and expectations of everyone, I have voluntarily become a servant to any and all in order to reach a wide range of people: religious, non-religious, meticulous moralists, loose-living moralists, the defeated, the demoralised – whoever. I didn't take on their way of life. I kept my bearings in Christ – but I entered their world and tried to experience things from their point of view. I've become just about every sort of servant there is in my attempts to lead those I meet into a God-saved life. I did all this because of the Message. I didn't just want to talk about it; I wanted to be in on it.'

Many people in our local community see the church as irrelevant and past its sell by date. This is coupled with apathy in general terms that means only 30% of the electorate turn out to vote in an election. To engage with our local culture, it appears to me that there are key issues. In our community children are very important, as there are many young families. Our children's ministry will need someone to lead it in a full time capacity, to enable us to do things for the children outside the traditional

Sunday school activities. After school club will become important and an art club after school has been started already. Children's Church may have to have some activities on a Saturday morning to be able to have more children. These will be action-packed activity-based gatherings of children.

Worship for many is not engaging. And does it have to be on a Sunday? There are some churches that have started what have been called seeker services. However, yet again we expect people to come to us. The gospel must be incarnated and because of the gap between church culture and the society around us, this is becoming more demanding and risky.

This is something that must again not be the responsibility of one person. This is one of the greatest challenges in our day, especially because of the cynicism there is in our culture towards the church and the religiosity we often are seen to represent. The people in the pews will have to be part of this journey of discovery. Listening to those who are part of the church and to those who are not part of the church will be very important.

In the context of Northern Ireland there is also the issue of how we relate to other denominations. The ecumenical movement is just bad news to many people. The division between Catholic and Protestant is so profoundly deep and painful for many that involving people in this journey is difficult and risky. In our parish we have been part of a four church fellowship that has helped us meet with other Christians on a regular basis. Lay people have led this and they have organised the programmes. The most helpful evenings have been when we have heard from the different denominations about what they view as the main issues facing the church today. These are small steps but steps that have to be taken in such a divided country, where polarisation has been much more focused. 'How has it come about that the vast majority of Protestant Christians are content to see the Church of Jesus Christ split up into hundreds of separate sects, feel no sense of shame about such a situation, and sometimes even glory in it and claim the support of the New Testament for it?' (*The Household of God,* Leslie Newbigin, page 54.) This is a painful journey for us all but it is one we must travel for the sake of the kingdom. I believe the integrity of the gospel is at stake if we do not seek to bring healing to ancient hurts.

During the past ten years there has also been the growing number of young retired people in our parish. There are those who have chosen to retire early and there are those who have had to. There is an ever-increasing band of very able and experienced people who have time to offer support and help. This is an opportunity to discover new ministries and opportunities for service. Many of these people in our context have already started to help with a ministry to our elderly and housebound, although there may be reluctance from some to become too tied down until they see how this retirement business works out. This is another reason for releasing people into ministry rather than keeping the structure that we have under such control that again only the ordained person can minister.

There is also a greater number of elderly people who need to be shown that the church has not forgotten them. Old age for many can become something bleak and foreboding, although I visit a lady who is over one hundred years old who tells me she is only suffering from 'youth deficiency' and not old age. 'Senior citizens are often overlooked in our youth-orientated, age-sensitive and death-denying culture ... Further many are discovering that living longer does not always mean enjoying carefree golden years ... The ageing process can be a discomforting experience, with failing strength and faculties, and increased health problems that drain resources. The fragmentation of the family means that churches will be called upon to provide increasing support.' (*Church Next*, Coffey and Gibbs, page 221.) We have had a team of parish visitors who for some time visit some of our housebound parishioners. It was a former curate who started this under a previous rector. It is still helping and has now been supplemented with a regular service of Holy Communion in the parish hall followed by lunch and some entertainment. This is a simple and yet important way that the body of Christ can minister to one another.

Two other areas in church life today that are of importance are our children and our young people. I have already discussed some of the issues surrounding children and worship but as important is the question of Sunday School. This is a subject I have struggled with for some time. I worry that the model we are still trying to function with has not changed during my lifetime. The group of children is taught by one person who gives information and knowledge to a group of passive (wishful thinking) children. The teacher is often a teenager who is there because it may be difficult to get other volunteers. We have recently moved from a Sunday School model to a children's church model. This is much more interactive, participatory and fun. Activities and games are part of this model although already it is obvious there is just not enough time on Sunday mornings. As we have reflected upon our practice we are moving towards the idea of having someone with expertise and training to lead this important ministry. We may have to look at Saturday morning or after school activities to engage with our children because of the learning culture they now experience and because of the changing culture of Sundays. However, staffing and facilitating such activities will be a problem.

Within the area of youth ministry I feel very old and inadequate. We have appointed a full time youth worker in our setting for the past five years. This has been a very important development. Volunteers who did a very good job had staffed it for a long time. Now the volunteers can be supported, trained, resourced and affirmed by someone working alongside them. I believe it has also helped our young people feel affirmed by having their own member of staff. It has also removed the burden of this responsibility from the curate who would often be landed with this task whether they were gifted in this area or not. In my youth in the church I remember that my peers and I were given somewhere to meet and the chance to meet together. Belonging to my peer group and having something to do was critical.

In the many areas I have raised there are issues of training and facilitating that will have to be addressed for any developments to happen. As I look forward to my ministry I am even more conscious than ever that there is no clear plan or guide to follow. There is the need to be flexible and to think creatively. This has to be done in a world that is full of paradox. There are no guarantees that we will not make mistakes or that people will not misunderstand what we are trying to do. However, we will have to take risks in parish ministry if we are not going to continue to manage decline.

I want to share the leadership I have been entrusted with. I want to learn to trust one of the greatest gifts I have been given and that is the people of God. I look forward to the journey, not because I know the destination, but because I have some wonderful companions on the journey, and he has promised to be with us.

CHAPTER 12

To teach or to train

Discontent among those who have received any form of professional training appears to be guaranteed. To hear unrestrained praise and contentment from anyone who has undergone such training is highly unusual. Certainly within the Church of Ireland part of the clergy's lot appears to be dissatisfaction with the training for ordination. It is almost obligatory to have a good moan. It has been discussed in various places and unfortunately some of what has been said has been very negative and personal.

In remembering my own college days and the training I received, I am left with some very important friendships that have been invaluable to me on my journey. These friends have become soul friends and they have taught me about different experiences of faith and about a variety of spiritualities. There can be a special bond between those who share the same vocational struggle, between those who are trying to live out that vocation within the confines of the institutional church, with all its fulfilment and frustration.

As well as the friendships I gained, I also learned the value of regular, disciplined and daily prayer. There were many times, for me, when it was boring, rigid and restrictive, because I had to do it. However, it was a pattern that I have learned to value and I have found it comforting and even critical to my survival, when I was struggling to keep my vocation alive.

I will be forever grateful to those who helped shape and mould me at a formative stage of my ministry. Their ability to cope with my frustration and anger at the structures of church life have obviously borne fruit, in that I am still on that journey.

However, if I had the chance to offer some kind of blueprint for training today there are some key issues I would want to address. The following thoughts are an attempt to put these ideas together in the hope that they might stimulate discussion on such a very important matter. There is a great danger in church life that we continue to do what we have always done rather than find creative ways of doing it better.

In the time I have had to put these thoughts together, I have found myself rediscovering what it was that started me on this journey. As a young student it was very clear and simple – I loved Jesus because he loved me. In an attempt to respond to him I felt called to ordination. The language here may not be helpful to some but it was how I saw it at the time. I wanted to share his love with others. Over the years of ordained ministry, it has been difficult at times to remember where it all began. The constant involvement in the pain of others, coping with the frustrations of the institutional church, dealing with the expectations of the religious people and the great sense of inadequacy meant that my vocation took a battering. There were times when the job advertisements in various newspapers became very attractive. Vocation does get damaged in the process of following it and I know one of the great dangers of clerical life is cynicism. It is the need to protect and guard this fragile plant of vocation that would be my first suggestion for training.

In my own experience since ordination, spiritual direction is the element in my own journey that has helped me find resources to keep this plant alive. Even though there would be resistance I believe that every candidate for ordination should receive spiritual direction. Students for the ministry should be given resources, new ways of praying and new aids to keeping alive the essence of what brought them to ordination in the first place. There are not enough staff in the college to do this but there are others in the wider church who could help with it. This would also help students from different backgrounds and experiences to learn something of the value of other people's spirituality, especially when it is different from their own. There is the danger in college that students only really keep the company of those they agree with and they do not learn to handle the very real differences there are in our religious culture and church life.

In my own experience I went to college with an evangelical background, a charismatic experience and a resistance to anything catholic. I needed help to realise that at heart I am a contemplative. I am someone who likes retreats, silence, and spiritual direction and yet maintains a love of scripture and a use of spiritual gifts. The richness and diversity of spiritual disciplines has helped keep vocation alive. It has also helped me appreciate others, especially those who express their faith in different ways from me. The most important place for the resources to protect the spiritual life to be learnt and to be put in place is during the training, so that habits and disciplines are established before the battering of religious life begins.

One of the key lessons in this spiritual awareness has been the value of contemplation. This was alien to my own background and it is something I discovered years after my ordination. 'Prayer is a rhythmic movement of our personality into the eternity and peace of God and no less into the turmoil of the world for whose sake as for ours we are seeking God. If this is the heart of prayer, then the contemplative part of it will be large. And a church which starves itself and its members in the contemplative life deserves whatever spiritual leanness it may experience.' (*Canterbury Pilgrim*, Michael Ramsey, pages 59-60.)

This contemplation has helped me take stock, it has helped me to stop doing ministry and allow myself time to be. From my own Protestant background I inherited a great desire to do, to help, to be with people and to sort out their lives for them. I have had to learn that at times I just need to be, to take time to reflect and to be still. 'Contemplation comprises the huge realities of worship and prayer without which we become performance-driven and program-obsessed pastors. A contemplative life is not an alternative to the active life, but its root and foundation … The contemplative life generates and releases an enormous amount of energy into the world – the enlivening energy of God's grace rather than the enervating frenzy of our pride.' (*Under the Unpredictable Plant*, Eugene Peterson, pages 114-115.)

Spiritual direction is therefore given to help students, at the formative stage of their vocational journey, to find the resources and spirituality that will help keep that vocation alive amidst the frustration and fulfilment that lies ahead of them.

From my own memory of training, and in discussing training with many people who have trained for ordination, there is a particular theological issue that is at the core of some of the difficulties people experience. 'It surfaces as a pastoral question of how to "apply" the scientific results of historical critical studies (of the Bible) to contemporary pastoral practice and preaching.' (*But She Said*, Elizabeth Fiorenza, page 174.) For many in the process of training there is a great tension with this subject of biblical criticism. This is the study of the texts of the Bible and how we received them. What, if any, is the original text? Who wrote the original text we have? How can we be sure the texts are trustworthy? Do any of the gospel accounts give us the actual words of Jesus? These are difficult and complex issues. One of the dangers is that anyone with a passionate belief in scripture is dismissed as fundamentalist in a disparaging way. This does not help people to be receptive to learning. Others can be left wondering what authority scripture has for preaching and teaching, which is part of the ordination vows.

When biblical theology is detached from preaching and the use of the Bible it becomes a very arid and dull subject. The relevance of any biblical theology needs to be applied at all times. This would be much easier to do if certain other options were looked at, such as an apprenticeship training that keeps students in a parish situation as they are learning these academic subjects. To remove theology from pastoral practice often means it is very difficult for students to put the two together again.

This perhaps is the nub of my own thinking on this subject. I believe ordination training that takes place as a student works in a parish context would give a much more rounded approach to training to do the job. Parish placements and summer placements have helped but much of the real learning and teasing out of the issues happen when they are being faced in the actual parish setting. Academic learning must be related to the context and this at present is only done after ordination when many students have questioned the relevance of the training because it has been removed from that context.

With the present model of training it is virtually impossible to assess how students will perform in the ministry. There is an assessment in academic ability but not in the ability to do the job that is required after ordination. Ministry today is increasingly about being able to think creatively and plan strategically for the future, otherwise we are simply managing decline. 'Ordained ministry, as a practice, is learned by imitation rather than by mere exchange of information. Seminaries may even be the wrong venue for such discipleship to take place. Apprenticeship might be far the better route.' (*Shaping our Future*, Freeman, page 41.)

Theological colleges are rather unusual places, in my mind. They resemble a boarding school environment. There is the strict framework of study and community living, with a structure of daily prayer. Inherent in this model is the danger that mature students are treated like children rather than as future leaders in the church. Married students are asked to live apart from their families. The families are left to cope with this as part of the cost of the call, even though they are not called to ordination. This can and does create resentment, especially when the institution itself espouses the values of family life. This model of seminary training allows no flexibility; it does not allow for different people with different needs and gifts to train in a variety of ways. The church in general has always found it difficult to cope with untidiness and variety.

If this seminary model could be replaced by an apprenticeship, whereby students spent short blocks of time in a college environment but most of the time in a parish setting for their training, some of these issues could be addressed. A model that allows for training in a specific situation appears to be in use in every other profession in our society, yet we still insist on a model of training that separates students from the actual context in which they are called to work. A critical part of this model would be the ability to train people how to work as part of a team rather than as a one-person band. They could learn to equip others and learn to be assessed by the people they are seeking to minister to and with. 'The church leaders of tomorrow have been trained in a competitive environment where private study is at the heart of the learning experience – a habit that is hard to break. Where does the individual student learn to work with a team of peers in addressing issues, dividing tasks and achieving group consensus? These skills are not developed by sitting in straight rows in a lecture room environment and working in a cubicle in the library.' (*Church Next*, Coffey and Gibbs, page 108.)

The seminary model also raises questions that lie at the heart of any adult education process. 'One of the major problems is that the generally conceived notion of education amongst adults current in Britain is one which implicitly assumes that the teacher knows and the learner doesn't. It is therefore commonly seen as the task of the teacher to transmit what he knows into that vacuum of the mind of the learner … It is an inappropriate model for education in faith and discipleship, in which there is the need to consider and reflect upon the individual's experience.' (ACCM paper 18, October 1988.) The rich diversity of the students training for the ordained ministry brings a wealth of experience and wisdom that can be used by the students to teach each other. This style of learning is best done as people reflect upon their learning and experience in a context of parish life. Summer schools and weekend residentials can bring this wealth of learning into focus, as students are given structured learning to help them work out the issues that they have had to encounter. This model of learning also follows the principle that reflection and learning do not stop at ordination.

In the same ACCM paper the following is said: 'A theological education for professional ministry which is dominated by the need to pass on received traditions in terms of verbal formulae and isolated textual criticism not only transmits philosophical understandings of the being of God, but also transmits an implicit understanding that the study of theology is detached from living faith and is primarily concerned with handling such formulae with dexterity.' (Ibid.) One of the developments since my own ordination is the increase of the number of ordinands who come from a previous occupation. I went straight from school to university to theological college. The experience people now bring to their training means they have acquired skills and insights that are helpful when shared with others in training. They also bring a refreshing view from the pews. One of the dangers with the seminary model is that we try to produce a standard model of the clergy. We are to dress the same, speak the same, and think the same. This is a parody of what happens but perhaps there is a grain of truth in it. The greatest gift anyone brings to their ordination is the gift of their own life and experience.

Much of my own thinking on this subject has been shaped by looking at new models of training now being offered in certain parts of the Church of England. I had the privilege of spending some time with some of the students from the South Western Ministry Course (SWMTC), and they were very welcoming and hospitable. They were delighted to have someone who could teach them the words of 'Danny Boy' during their impromptu concert on a Saturday evening.

These students were using a model of training more akin to an apprenticeship model. They were not in a seminary but they did meet together regularly throughout the year in small tutorial groups, they attended classes in the local university, they had residential weekends and various 'summer schools' that were also residential. They were placed in a parish context under supervision. The people supervising them were trained to be part of this process. If their own parish context was unsuitable then an alternative parish was agreed. There were tensions in this model of balancing work, study and family life. There were some students who had given up paid employment and others who could not afford to do so. For their families there was less upheaval, although that would come at the time of ordination when they would move to their curacy.

For these students it was the style of learning that brought about the most favourable comments. The methodology was very important. They were learning so much from each other as they together reflected on each other's parish situation with the learning they had been given as part of the academic teaching. People from many and varied backgrounds were able to share their expertise for the good of others. I was able to witness this in action in some of their small group work that they allowed me to share in. I found this very refreshing and stimulating. The discussions were constantly rooted in the parish context in which they shared.

I quote from the statement of belief and practice from SWMTC as it highlights the thinking behind this model of training. 'Ministry belongs to the church and not to the ordained, and therefore there can be no ministry that should not be exercised interdependently and collaboratively. Despite much fine work on this … the reality is often vastly different from the theory. The ordained are often a significant part of the problem, not the solution. This is partly because of the roles and responsibilities they are asked to exercise, which sometimes fit awkwardly with a genuinely mutual and collaborative ministry; partly because expectations are powerfully present about "traditional" roles being maintained – the call for strong leaders is not confined to politics and schools, but can be found in the churches as well; and partly because the ordained have insufficient awareness of the ways in which their personal needs and desires shape the exercise of their ministry. We are committed to preparing people for interdependent and inter-animative practices of ministry, and believe that a key aspect of this is understanding of and good practice in working in groups. Genuine meeting between people is part of how we try, tentatively, to understand the life of God as Trinity. Only to the extent of being fully present to others in this way can the minister "bear reality" and go any significant way towards incarnating the presence and concerns of God. Only with a deep understanding of groups and their part in them can ministers begin to make best use of the opportunities of their work in which groups feature so largely. (SWMTC statement of belief and practice, par 19.)

The emphasis on group work is something students found difficult but helpful. There were very real tensions because of personality clashes, theological differences and cultural backgrounds. Course tutors led these groups very skilfully and they were modelling something that is very important in parish life. As I reflect on my ministry, I would have found this helpful in how to handle small groups and also how to handle conflict in these groups, which seemed to be part of the experience of these students. As I witnessed this model, students were not being *taught* but *trained*.

I also visited Sarum College in Salisbury, where the Southern Theological and Training Scheme (STETS) is based. One of the facets of both these training models is that they are ecumenical. Training within these settings recognises that there are many and varied ministries that people need trained for. STETS has also moved away from the seminary model and is based on the same scheme of components as SWMTC.

'The STETS programme is designed for adults and, therefore, takes seriously what you already know about the Christian faith, through your participation in the life of the church as well as your prior study. Educationally it provides you with ways of relating what you already know to wider perspectives drawn from the whole Christian tradition. It also gives you a wide range of opportunities for training and formation to enable you to become a skilled ministerial practitioner and to "embody" your skills within the church of God.

Thus at STETS you will find you do theology as much through taking part in Christian worship or engaging with specific aspects of society as through critical study of the Christian tradition or even of how people know what they know.' (STETS course handbook, page 4.)

In these models there is great flexibility, in that students can choose certain optional modules as well as studying a core curriculum. Depending on personal circumstances, modules can be taken when it is suitable for the student. For families this non-seminary model helps them stay in their own home and retain some kind of normal family life. In this model the whole church is involved in training because it is based in a parish context. The parish has to find ways of helping and affirming the students and taking responsibility for them. The testing of vocation in a particular situation enables people to become more excited about ordination or it may help some discover it is not for them. The New Testament shows ministry being tested and tried in a local situation before it is recognised by the wider church. 'Is there any good reason for removing all who might be used by God in ministry for three years from their local church setting, filling their minds with theology (much of which they may never need to use in their daily work), and sending them to serve their apprenticeship in an area they probably know nothing about? In the early church the leaders were nearly always appointed where they served. They had the advantage of knowing the local scene intimately, and were therefore naturally placed for fulfilling an effective pastoral and preaching ministry according to the gifts given to them by God.' (*I Believe in the Church*, David Watson, pages 267-268.)

At present students are placed in parishes for weekends and various summer placements. Having had students do this in our parish, they have proved very beneficial to all, not least because the students are better equipped to reflect upon what they have learned in the context of the parish.

Another key element in the STETS and SWMTC programmes is reflective practice. 'We want you to learn to connect thought and practice in rigorous, creative and prayerful ways, so that you may come to a critical awareness of what you are doing and why you are doing it and of how your actions fit into the mission of the church.' (STETS course handbook, page 2.) In the busyness of ministry it is very difficult to reflect upon what you are doing because it is easier just to do it. The habit of reflection needs to be established, and in training is the obvious time to do this.

Having had time away from the parish to reflect upon my own ministry, I have been very conscious of exhaustion at having been doing so much. I have found the task of caring for so many people at different points of their lives very draining. There have been times when I have simply performed in professional mode. I cannot change what goes on around me, but having had time to reflect I can change my behaviour in the midst of the busyness. This idea of reflective practice is also meant to teach the students that reflection is always an essential part of ministry. This does not end when we are ordained. We can never say we have finished our training because we must continue to assess and learn as we offer ourselves in ministry. The present seminary model has the inherent danger of implying that training finishes at ordination or at the end of a curacy. There are no other professions that would allow people to continue to practice their profession without further training. 'The value of in-service training cannot be over emphasised ... If the God-given gifts and ministries are to develop for the benefit of the whole church, the fresh stimulation from continuous study, coupled with an ever-ready willingness to learn, is vital. We are all disciples, or learners, to the end of our days.'(*I Believe in the Church*, D. Watson, page 268.)

In attempting to summarise these thoughts on training, I do so with the preface that there is no such thing as the perfect model for training. However, there are some central issues to this subject as I see it. Those who come to be ordained need to be given the resources to keep alive the very life that brought them to the point of training for ordination. I think some form of spiritual direction best does this. Spiritual direction can help people develop their own rule of life. It can help them discover different ways of praying and relate their devotional life to their personality and needs.

There is the issue of helping students find ways of relating academic study of the Bible to preaching and teaching. This is probably best done by moving away from the seminary model to the apprenticeship model of training. This allows for academic study to be earthed in the actual context in which ministry will be exercised in the parish. This can be supplemented with residential schools and weekends and this can still be offered through any faculty of theology. The nature of parish life has changed so much in my lifetime, and the needs faced by those who are ordained so much more complex, that this is an imperative for the future training of clergy.

The title I gave to this chapter highlights the overall idea I want to capture in this discussion. Students for the ordained ministry must be trained and not just taught. This training must encapsulate the principle that training is for life and does not end at ordination. I have found it very valuable looking at other models of training for the ministry. I trust these thoughts will help others discuss this subject, in such a way that the whole church may help all who offer themselves for ordination in whatever denomination to fulfil their God-given potential amidst the frustration that exists in being part of the church.

CHAPTER 13

More than Survival

As I mentioned in a previous chapter, I had various struggles very early in my ministry with my spirituality. I had inherited the 'quiet time', daily readings and prayer, but found that it was not enough of a resource to help me face the enormous challenge and demand of public ministry. I began at an early stage to search for new elements to help me on my spiritual journey.

During the last few years I have been able to piece together snippets of information about my father that I didn't know before. I was amazed to find out things about his past. The discoveries have been exhilarating and disturbing. For the early years of his childhood he lived no more than one hundred yards from where we have lived for the last ten years. He went to the same school as my children are attending. These and other details have left me with more unanswered questions.

The same is true with the various discoveries I have made in my spiritual journey over the last twenty years. In searching for things that would help me more than just survive ordination, some of them have helped me and some have disturbed me, although being disturbed has often led to growth and made me move beyond some misconceptions.

In our culture it is very difficult to find silence. Whether we are shopping in a supermarket, pursuing sport in a leisure centre, sailing in a ferry, flying in an aeroplane, or eating in a café or restaurant, there is music or noise coming at us from all directions. Shopping centres, telephones and cars all have music to enable us to shop, wait or travel. The personal stereo can even destroy a quiet walk by the sea or in the country. Silence appears to unsettle or question the hectic pace of living.

Dallas Willard comments: 'In silence we close off our souls from "sounds", whether those sounds be noise, music or words. Total silence is rare, and what we today call "quiet" usually only amounts to a little less noise. Many people have never experienced silence and do not even know that they do not know what it is. Our households and offices are filled with the whirring, buzzing, murmuring, chattering, and whining of the multiple contraptions that are supposed to make life easier. Their noise comforts us in some curious way. In fact we find complete silence shocking because it leaves the impression that nothing is happening. In a go-go world such as ours, what could be worse than that?' (*The Spirit of Disciplines*, D. Willard, page 163.)

In the revelation of scripture, silence appears to be viewed as a struggling with the presence of God. Silence is a creative part of God's revelation throughout the ages. This creativity of silence should be an important part of any spiritual journey. Before the created order came into being there was a void, emptiness, and a silence, and out of this God created. In the wilderness experience there was the struggle of God's people to know and love him and they were commanded to 'Be silent.' (Deuteronomy 27:9.) Elijah tried to flee from the task God had given him but he discovered God in the 'gentle whisper' or 'the still small voice'. (1 Kings 19:9-13.) In the vision that Isaiah received as part of his call there was the silence produced by God's holiness. (Isaiah 6:1-6.) In Psalm 4 we are encouraged to 'search our hearts and be silent.' (Psalm 4: 4.) As we reflect upon the birth narratives in the gospels, I believe there is the silence of the incarnation. If we had been organising this event, we would have employed a good public relations company to inform the world's media. God announced it with a few shepherds, who were of little importance in their society, some strangers from the East and a choir of angels. In the words of a Christmas hymn:

'How silently, how silently,
the wondrous gift is given!'
(*O Little town of Bethlehem*, Philip Brooks.)

In the midst of the events surrounding the birth is the awful unspeakable tragedy of the 'holy innocents'. Throughout the ministry that Jesus exercised he is silent on his identity and person. It is interesting to note that before Pilate 'he made no reply'. (Matthew 27:14.) There was the silence of those around him and how they also left him alone. Initially the silence of the empty tomb left the disciples fearful and confused. Silence is an integral part of God's revelation as we have it. Even today the only response that we are left with as we face suffering is silence. When we ask about reasons for why things happen, the only answer is the wall of silence. We need to discover the silence within, where we can discern the 'gentle whisper' of God.

I had assumed that prayer and Bible reading developed my inner life. This idea of being still and the creativity of silence opened up new avenues of God's grace. In the silence I became more aware of the great struggle taking place within me. In the silence I was able to hear words of help to soothe my fears and insecurities. I need this space to listen to the voice within; it enables me to find a quiet centre within the busyness of doing. There was a danger that, even in my praying, I was doing rather than being.

'The busier life is, the more there is need for a still centre; a place deep within us to which we can withdraw after the day-to-day buffeting and storms; a place where we can reflect on experience and try and make sense of life; a place where we can mull over events and savour them more fully; a place where, above all, we can listen ... to what others are saying verbally and non-verbally, to what our feelings and fears are saying to us, and to what God is saying through circumstances, through people, through creation and his word spoken in the depths of our being. All these things pass by, like views from the window of an express train, if we do not stand still at disciplined intervals and do some stock-taking and viewing.' (*Jesus Man of Prayer*, Sister Mary Magdalene, page 40.)

Over the years I have come to need this silence more and more. In the silence I can find affirmation and peace. I can find the patient loving father whom I seek to serve encouraging me to be me. I do not have to become somebody else, or have certain theological views, or be a wonderfully skilled rector. I am called to be me. So much of my early Christian experience was about being good enough, trying to do my best and ensuring I did not let him down. I cannot and will never earn God's love – it is simply given as a gift. I can imagine the father running towards me as I wait before him. The silence is part of my journey where I have begun to experience freedom in being a child of God, the person he has called me to be.

This gift of silence is often associated with solitude in the various spiritual writings of many of those who have been on the same inner journey. Solitude is the place where we can find space and quiet to be alone in silence with God. Thomas à Kempis, as he discovered the monastic call, wrote: 'Shut thy door upon thee and call thee to Jesus thy love: dwell with him in thy cell for thou shalt not find elsewhere so great peace.' (Quoted in *The Spirit of Disciplines,* Dallas Willard, page 162.) During this sabbatical, apart from time with my family most weekends, I have been on my own. I have found that silence and solitude very enriching. For the first time in twenty years I found myself praying for me and not for others. Over this extended period away from doing, I have had quality time to be with God.

In the cut and thrust of parish ministry, it is essential that we build in places of silence and solitude. From time to time we need to escape from the demands, the noise, the activity, the praying and be silent on our own before God. 'Action, planning, desiring are all suspended … while the thoughts and emptiness and realities that surround them are given a chance to regroup.' (*The Other Side of Silence,* M. Kelsey, page 100.)

Henri Nouwen writes: 'Have you ever tried to spend a whole day doing nothing but listening to the voice that dwells deep in your heart? … It is not easy to enter in to the silence and reach beyond the many boisterous and demanding voices of our world and to discover the small intimate voice saying: "You are my Beloved Child, on you my favour rests." Still, if we dare to embrace our solitude and befriend our silence, we will come to know that voice. I do not want to suggest to you that one day you will hear that voice with your bodily ear. I am not speaking about a hallucinatory voice, but about a voice that can be heard by the ear of faith, the ear of the inner heart.' (*The Only Necessary Thing*, Henri Nouwen, page 84.) I am still on this journey of learning to hear the gentle whisper and at times it has been difficult and at times enriching.

As part of this journey I have also found the use of a journal very helpful. A journal is essentially a notebook. There are times when I have felt compelled to write a letter to God to express prayers that I have found impossible to put into speech. For some reason writing has been easier than speaking. 'A spiritual journal is an honest record of our experiences with God.' (*Spiritual Life*, J. Westerhoff, page 68-69.) The journal has been particularly helpful as I have journeyed through my past for healing. It has also helped when there are difficult decisions to be made. There are times when hell itself appears to have been let loose in the many crises in the lives of others. My journal has been of great benefit in these moments, putting my internal struggle with faith and God into words. The records of these various times are of help in seeing the ebb and flow of the inner life. They are like my own book of psalms. They therefore become a tool for recollection and remembering. This remembering is a biblical way of looking forward. As we remember how God has been with us in the past, it makes it easier to look to the future. Some people are very religious in the use of a journal and use it every day. However, it is something I can use, may use and do use, but do not have to use. Like all other spiritual disciplines, it is only an avenue of God's presence and peace.

From my own Protestant upbringing the subject of spiritual direction left me feeling uneasy at first. This would have been understood as a particularly Catholic practice and therefore not for me. Richard Foster comments: 'It is a beautiful expression of divine guidance through the help of our brothers and sisters.' (*The Celebration of Discipline*, R. Foster.) Many people receive this help in a formal arrangement with a spiritual director. In the early years of my ministry I decided to try this discipline. I wanted someone to help me in the busyness and demands of public ministry so that I would not forget to be a disciple.

There were times when I was first ordained I had difficulty in praying. I would go through the motions of saying my prayers but I found it extremely difficult to trust God. With the help of a director we were able to trace my difficulty to my childhood and my lack of relationship with my father. It was obvious that trust for me was always going to be hard. I was encouraged to reflect on my past and thus began a journey that was eventually to lead to me trying to trace my dad. Alongside this it was suggested that I should use some biblical passages for meditation, focusing on the amazing love God has expressed for all his children. This is why I have always found the image of the 'forgiving father' so poignant. With these and other insights I found myself having to re-think my perception of God. He was not always watching to see if I failed. He was not going to leave me to do it myself. There is no doubt in my mind that to walk these and other paths I needed the help of someone to walk them with me. My director has also encouraged me to experiment with other disciplines in my inner life. This has helped me feel that I am not just doing my duty.

I must say that I still find prayer very difficult. There are days when I cannot pray. There are days when I do not want to pray. There are days when I wonder if I am living a lie.

A definition of spiritual direction may help those who may still feel nervous of what it is. 'First helping the directee pay attention to God as he reveals himself; second, helping the directee recognise his reactions and decide on his responses to God.' (*The Practice of Spiritual Direction*, Barry and Connolly, page 46.) Kenneth Leech puts this discipline in perspective: 'Spiritual direction is therefore a means to an end. The end is God, whose service is perfect freedom.' (*Soul Friend*, K. Leech, page 89.)

In the context of direction, another issue that has arisen is that of confession. Within the Anglican tradition it is often stated: 'All may, none must and some should.' In talking to someone else about my inner life it has been useful on occasions to ask for God's forgiveness and to hear someone pronounce the forgiveness that God promises. Alternatively it has been useful to write a confession and to burn the piece of paper as a reminder of God's forgiveness. 'As far as the east is from the west, so far has he removed our sins from us.' (Psalm 103:12.) Guilt is something that is difficult for those who are ordained, as we have to live with it all the time, feeling guilty for the many things we have not been able to do.

Support is essential in ministry because it can be a very lonely place. I have found it important to have a few trusted friends that I can share with. On this subject there may be disagreement as some of these friends would be parishioners. From my training I was always given to believe that we had to be very careful not to have friends in the parish. If people became friends then it would be difficult to pastor them; we should keep our distance. My personality cannot do this and I disagree with these sentiments. I will always share myself with those I work with and they usually respond in the same way. Therefore in parish ministry I have a few trusted friends I can talk to, laugh with and if needs be cry with. These are people who know me, who know the parish and whose judgement I can trust.

Beyond the parish I have also found it good to have a small group of clerical colleagues that I can talk to regularly. This kind of support has been labelled a 'triad'. This is a group of three people who meet every six to eight weeks. We as a group meet around an informal communion led by one of the group. Another member of the group leads our discussion, while the final member can talk about any issue they want to related to their ministry or parish. It has been liberating to realise that others experience the tensions and frustrations of ordained ministry.

All these various things I have found to be supports. This vocation is very demanding and my emotions are always in gear to attempt to empathise with those in need. There are times when the weight of expectations have made me feel I am the only person allowed to minister and this has been a difficult burden to carry. Yet I have also been told that I have brought people something of God's presence and peace and there is no greater reward than that. In this paradox of fulfilment and frustration, I have needed any support I can find to ensure that my vocation is kept alive. It was my relationship with Jesus in my teenage years that started this journey and that at times has taken a battering. Therefore I want to do all in my power to keep that relationship healthy. These supports have helped safeguard and protect this relationship. I do not want to just survive this ministry, I want to know that joy and peace that Jesus promises to those who follow him.

On a personal note I have found the love and support of my family invaluable. They are my greatest gift. They keep me humble, they help me experience love and acceptance. They are honest and affirming. Children are especially good at reminding me of my fallibility and humanness. Their banter and teasing, their fun and laughter are part of the rich tapestry that helps me be who I am.

There are great tensions in a rectory because of being in the public gaze. It is important for parishes to remember that the rectory family needs the rector as well. It is important for rectors to remember that their family needs cared for as well as all the other families. Holidays and days off are critical. We must find time to be available for our families and ourselves and we will in turn be of more help to others.

From a different perspective, we must look after the physical body as well. Exercise, sleep and diet contribute to our well being. In these weeks away from parish ministry I have lost weight, exercised more and slept better. In parish ministry there is the need to ensure that the body is cared for as in any other walk of life.

The mind must also be catered for. In ministry I have found it difficult to deal with anger and fear. Fear can paralyse us and make it impossible to do anything. It in effect numbs us. The journal is useful for facing any fears we may have and thus praying through them. Anger is a difficult emotion. There are times when it is all right to be angry but what we do with the anger is very important. A good game of tennis or a visit to Old Trafford helps me. It is dangerous not to deal with anger as it can explode or implode if we try to ignore it.

To keep myself physically and spiritually well on this journey is vital. The faith I started out with needs to be nurtured and developed. This faith will enable me to try new things, to go forward on this difficult journey, knowing he is with me. That conviction gives me the hope and vision to keep going and to be faithful to this incredible calling. However, I will always be on a journey and I will never be finished as I seek to minister to others. I pray for the strength and the faith to keep going. I also ask that those who share with me in ministry will continue to encourage and affirm me. I am more convinced than ever that in the ministry of the church we need to build one another up, although I also hope that we all can enjoy the journey with him and each other. It does help to have a sense of humour and not to take ourselves too seriously.

CHAPTER 14

The Journey Continues

These last few months that I have been given to write have been very special. I am writing this last chapter as I take a few days quiet on the island of Iona. What a beautiful place. This is the only place I have been where you can actually hear the silence. The quiet, the simplicity and the calm of God's creation that this place represents are very special. This island has links with so many people who have visited and prayed here and found they have left inspired. It is amazing to be in a place where people have prayed every day for centuries. To be caught up in the movement of history as pilgrims have come and gone from here for so long is very humbling. It has helped me regain a renewed perspective.

When we lived in Helen's Bay, I enjoyed travelling by train to Belfast for various meetings or hospital visits. The train helped me have time to read and not be in such a hurry. As I sat on the platform in Helen's Bay waiting for the train, I would often have a parable in my mind. The train would come from Bangor, stop for any passengers in Helen's Bay (unless it was the Belfast express), and then take us to our destination. It came from somewhere, stopped for passengers and then moved on again. It had a past, a present and a future. It was always in my mind a parable of my journey with Jesus. I had experienced, am experiencing and will experience his presence with me on my journey. Our faith must be three-dimensional. I have been saved through what he has done for me, I am being saved in the here and now and one day I will be saved when death comes. This is why I find the analogy of faith as a journey so helpful. 'Our real journey in life is interior: it is a matter of growth, a deepening and an ever greater surrender to the creative action of love and grace in our hearts.' (Thomas Merton quoted in *The Fire of Silence and Stillness*, P. Harris, page 12.)

As I have had time to reflect upon my journey of faith that has produced a vocation to the ordained ministry, I want to gather my thoughts together in a three dimensional way. I want to remember, to celebrate and to anticipate. I want to look back to the past, to pause in the present and to look forward to the future.

'God's call is mysterious ... it comes in the darkness of faith. It is so fine, so subtle, that it is only with the deepest silence within us that we can hear it. And yet nothing is so decisive and overpowering for a person on this earth, nothing surer or stronger. This call is uninterrupted: God is always calling us! But there are distinctive moments in this calling of his, moments which leave a permanent mark on us – moments which we can never forget.' (Carlo Carretto quoted in *The Fire of Silence and Stillness*, P. Harris, page 33.)

As I look back I am grateful to those who taught me that faith is something personal, alive and life changing. I give thanks for those who taught me to see the loveliness of Jesus. I found him in them. To those who loved me and helped me become who I am, again I am forever grateful. The people and parishes I have ministered with and in have shaped my thinking and praying. Some of that has been for good and some of it has caused me real struggle and pain. However, it is often in the struggle that I have been more aware of my dependency upon God. Therefore I can even be grateful for the struggles in ministry. There are many people who have affirmed my vocation by their actions and words; they will never know how much they have helped me on my journey. Affirmation is a powerful weapon in helping others. In the cut and thrust of parish life there have been those who have doubted me and been angry with me, they have helped me doubt myself and maybe be more open to criticism and appraisal. The past has been full of good and bad experiences, love and grief, joy and sorrow, faith and doubt; but in all of these experiences I have known that Jesus has been with me. The past has shaped me in so many ways and left various and important lessons. I cannot change any of my past but I can learn from it and I must not stay in the past. I am very aware from the culture that I grew up in that the past has often been held to be the only thing that matters. Too often there is the attempt by many to keep the community enslaved in the past. This is so destructive. Staying in the past is not an option if we want to grow and develop. As I look back to the influences upon my vocation, for the first time I am beginning to see my difficulty with the institutional church as a gift. It helps me struggle, question and be prepared to try to do things differently, even if that is somewhat cautiously.

I have just experienced his presence in a very moving and inspiring act of worship in the Abbey on Iona. There is a danger I do not want the present to become the past. This was a mountain top experience and, like Saint Peter, I want to stay here for a while. However, I cannot, these moments must become part of my past to encourage me to go forward.

'I urge you, then, pursue your course relentlessly. Attend to tomorrow and let yesterday be. Never mind what you have gained so far. Instead reach out to what lies ahead. If you do this you will remain in the truth. For now, if you wish to keep growing you must nourish in your heart the lively longing for God. Though this desire is certainly God's gift, it is up to you to nurture it … Press on then. I want to see how you fare. Our Lord is always ready. He only awaits your cooperation.' (*Cloud of Unknowing* quoted in *The Fire of Silence and Stillness*, P. Harris, page 122.)

It is good to be here but I cannot stay here. It is particularly important to be here today as it is the twentieth anniversary of my ordination. I have to begin a new chapter and new decade in ministry and I go forward renewed by this time out. In the context of Iona I have felt a renewed sense of call. It is a privilege to be called by God to this particular ministry. It is he who has called and it is he who enables me to do it. I have the difficult task of remaining faithful. This has been an important reminder of the present moment and that it is only in him that I can do what I have been called to do. So much of the present in ministry I spend being busy doing. I need to learn to rest in him. Jürgen Moltmann writes: 'We do not appropriate Christ for our use. We do not change him, but he changes us. We do not grasp him but he grasps us.' (Quoted by P. Harris, page 136.)

The future is always uncertain and with my past experiences I usually find the future most difficult. I can spend time worrying about what will never be. Fear has been defined as 'false expectations actually realised'. The old Anglo-Saxon root of the word anxiety is 'to be strangled'; to be pulled in one direction by our fears and in the opposite direction by our hopes. We are caught in the middle and thus we are strangled. I certainly need to learn not to waste energy worrying about something I cannot change. I want to look to the future with anticipation because it is part of my journey with Jesus. There is no map, some general directions but no guarantees that all will be as we would want it to be. We have the certain promise that he will be with us.

Some years ago I was reversing out of the garage and I heard the sound of crunching metal. When I got out of the car to inspect the damage, I found the front wheel of my bicycle with a few spokes broken. The wheel was not buckled and the axle was in place. The axle is so important to the wheel. It holds the rim, the spokes and the tyre all in place. They all revolve around the axle. The axle in turn is attached to the bicycle to make the wheel function.

One of the most important lessons in ministry is that I cannot do anything apart from him. The changes I would like to make to parish structures, the principle of shared leadership and ministry for all are certainly very important to me. If I focus only on all I want to do, I end up very frustrated and weary. Change happens very slowly in church life. I must not become so preoccupied with these issues that I lose sight of what brings me fulfilment. The axle is what keeps the vocation and faith in perspective. The focus must be on Jesus. 'You have not chosen me, but I have chosen you to go and bear fruit.' (John 15:16.) This is the real challenge of ministry, whether ordained or not. The most important lesson for me in this journey is described by Thomas Merton as follows: 'In the spiritual life there are no tricks and short cuts ... One cannot begin to face the life of prayer and meditation unless one is first perfectly content to be a beginner and really experience oneself as one who knows little or nothing, and has a desperate need to learn the bare rudiments. Those who think they "know" from the beginning never, in fact, come to know anything ... We do not want to be beginners. But let us be convinced of the fact that we will never be anything else but beginners, all our life.' (Quoted in P. Harris, page 182.)

So as a beginner I prepare to go into the future, with him who has called me, knowing that he has promised to be with me. I trust that as you read these thoughts they will help you on your journey with him. I have found his promise to be true. 'I'll be with you as you do this, day after day after day, right up to the end of the age.' (The Message, Matthew 28:30.)